Angel of Fear

ALBERT BUHR

Metta Press

Copyright © 2016 Albert Buhr

All rights reserved.

No part of this book may be reproduced in any form or by any means electronic or mechanical, including photocopying, recording, or by any information storage and retrieval system or technologies now known or later developed, without permission in writing from the publisher.

ISBN: 978-0-620-73314-4

Cover design and photo: Metta Press
Author photo: Shirene Briell

DEDICATION

To my daughter Mae,
and all the unseen hands giving guidance

CONTENTS

Introduction   1

PART 1: UNDERSTANDING FEAR

1. See Paris First   5
2. Swimming with Sharks   11
3. Tooth and Claw   17
4. The Nature of Fear   25

PART 2: KEYS TO ACCEPTANCE

5. Ground Control   35
6. Paradigm Shift   43
7. When Panic Attacks   55

PART 3: FREEDOM FROM FEAR

8. Love's Labours	73
9. Riding Lions	87
10. Compassion Cures	103
11. Angels and Demons	115
Appendix A – *"I'm Going Slightly Mad" by Rob Nairn*	119
Appendix B – *Orientation for Severe Anxiety*	125
Appendix C – *Recommended Reading*	127
Acknowledgments	131
About the Author	132

INTRODUCTION

Let me guess: the prospect of reading a book about fear doesn't fill you with *joie de vivre*. Nope, you want self-help bang for your buck – inspiration and mountaintops and everything better by Wednesday. Not swamplands and surrender.

It's natural to feel aversion in the vicinity of fear. Fear *is* aversion. But the greater gifts come from the muck and murk. Nightmares are rich in revelation.

Anxiety is a call to transformation – a view not easily found in our medicalized culture. Far from being a psychiatric illness, I contend that, for us as individuals, anxiety signals a potential evolution of consciousness. And if you suffer like I did, at the coalface of personal experience, this is more than theoretical. It gives courage. As our understanding expands, fear shrinks.

While this book may be an unusual ode to anxiety, it is also practical. With each chapter, it offers simple, pragmatic techniques and mental exercises for restoring your balance without recourse to the reductionist remedies that have become the default Freud-and-Prozac approach. By following these guidelines, you will build your resilience to remarkable levels, brick by brick. I was once suicidal with anxiety; today I feel fantastic – most of the time – and as calm as a Hindu cow.

You are invited to face fear and see it from multiple vantage points. For my workshops over the years, I have found that an integral method is most effective for the participants, because while there are biological correlates to our anxiety or depression, there are simultaneously cultural, psychological, interpersonal and spiritual dimensions at play.

So, "do not distress yourself with dark imaginings." The news is good. The route is clear. And let's have a little fun along the way.

Fearing Paris by Marsha Truman Cooper

Suppose that what you fear could be trapped and held in Paris.
Then you would have the courage to go everywhere in the world.
All the directions of the compass open to you,
except the degrees east or west of true north that lead to Paris.

Still, you wouldn't dare put your toes smack dab on the city limit line.
You're not really willing to stand on a mountainside, miles away,
and watch the Paris lights come up at night.

Just to be on the safe side, you decide to stay completely out of France.
But then the danger seems too close even to those boundaries,
and you feel the timid part of you covering the whole globe again.

You need the kind of friend who learns your secret and says,
"See Paris first."

PART 1: UNDERSTANDING FEAR

1

SEE PARIS FIRST

By noon, therapists were going door to door to counsel those who had witnessed the attack. A chopper hovered above the bay while the crew of two boats gazed into the water in a grim search for human remains.

The great white shark that had swallowed the 77-year-old grandmother was described as "the size of a helicopter." The searchers would find nothing. The only evidence of the event: a swimming cap washed up on the sand.

I was renting a refurbished fisherman's cottage on a mountainside on Cape Town's southern peninsula, penning my way into a new career as a travel writer. I had recently left a treadmill life in London, generally sleep-deprived and irreversibly bald after years of stress and urban overload, and was realizing my dream: to have a balcony-based home office under an umbrella, overlooking beautiful False Bay.

When the friendly trauma counsellor came knocking, I thanked her for the concern but confessed I had still been asleep when the tragedy happened that morning. I hadn't seen a thing. My early-rising neighbours were not so lucky.

I did not imagine it then, but within a few years I would find my calling also coaching others through trauma, stress and fear. My own severe struggles with panic and anxiety had at that time just begun.

The Most Important Thing

We are never told why Jacob wrestled with the angel, but it is no great mystery. Jacob was human after all, and as the poet Rilke noted, "every angel is terrifying."

In the book of Genesis, Jacob is on a journey to reconcile with his estranged brother. Alone on the banks of a river, he encounters a mysterious stranger, and a physical struggle ensues that lasts the night. The foe wounds Jacob, incapacitating him. Yet paradoxically, in his defeat he is victorious, and as the sun rises he realizes he has had a close encounter with the divine. He is given a new name, and senses that he has been fighting an angel.

The story is rich with the elements of a spiritual awakening. It starts with a tone of estrangement – a sense of having lost touch with kin. There is the struggle through the dark night of the soul, then surrender, which opens to an enlarged sense of mystery. The enemy, from a new perspective in the light of dawn, is recognised as an angelic ally. The passage is a brief but brilliant description of personal transformation.

Unbearable stress and anxiety is our great collective call to transformation. It has reached epidemic proportions, possibly unprecedented in the history of the world.

The philosopher Søren Kierkegaard said that knowing anxiety and learning from it is *"the most important thing"* and that it is our "best teacher." Heidegger and Sartre agreed that it is *the* primary emotion. Our friend Freud called it "the nodal point at which the most various and important questions converge, a riddle whose solution would be bound to throw a flood of light upon our whole mental existence."

For some, fear escalates to a level of anxiety that gives their days a nightmare quality. It can hammer them so hard that reality itself feels unreal, and they feel haunted. There is menace and madness in every direction, and the overwhelming sense that everything is about to go horribly wrong. They face each day with vague yet serious misgivings – like their very survival is on the line.

After a stressful lifestyle saw me pack some of life's larger shifts into the space of a few months, the real burden that led to burnout and breakdown was my constant indulgence in worry. Moving back to Cape Town from London, buying a house, then the 2008 financial meltdown, getting married, a pregnancy to follow soon thereafter, as well as a thrilling case of undiagnosed tick-bite fever leading to pancreatitis, all became the classic "full catastrophe." These events drove my nervous system to the edge – my operating system said "don't happy, be worry."

For what seemed like an endless dark night, I struggled to get rid of a crippling and unshakeable anxiety that invaded my mind and body. If I managed to sleep at all, I would wake at dawn with heart palpitations and watch the duvet on my chest shudder. In the dead of night I tried to Google my way out of nightmares. Drenched in the relentless rush of adrenaline for weeks without end, I grit my teeth in white-knuckle determination while waiting in grocery-store queues, wallowing in the *what ifs*, drinking deep from the wells of dread. Paralysed by panic, I felt beaten down, mauled and tortured, and stuck with *the worst thing of all*.

But in the end, it was actually one of the *best things*. It was the labour preceding my own slow rebirth – slow, because transformation is a process, not an event. Stress, panic, worry, anxiety… these are all merely amplified expressions of fear. My own inner ordeal has given me an invaluable understanding of this primary emotion, and how to relate to it. Carl Jung writes: "In psychology one possesses nothing unless one has experienced it in reality. Hence a purely intellectual insight is not enough, because one knows only the words and not the substance of the thing in itself."

My years in the vortex of fear taught me more than I could ever have imagined. So be warned, this book is full of the worst vice – advice. But here's the crux of it: when this apparent calamity befalls us, it is actually auspicious. There is no doubt that an ally, beyond the narrow scope of our embattled minds, has come to wrestle with us. Fear is the calling card of potential transformation.

LET'S DO IT ♦ Magic Magnesium

There is no magic bullet when it comes to curing anxiety. Believe me: if there were, I would be selling that miracle pill, not writing a book!

It's true, chemical tranquilizers, also known as anxiolytics (like alprazolam, or trademarks Xanax, Ativan, Klonopin, Serax, etc.) mostly work as advertised. Within minutes they block your body from registering adrenaline. This can be a huge relief when you've been relentlessly battered by your own hormones for days on end. But that is still a far cry from a cure. Anxiolytics are not happy pills – in fact, they may make you slightly depressed and give you a "flatland" feeling, conferring a counterfeit calm at best, not a genuine sense of tranquillity. They are highly addictive, and to stop taking them after any regular use usually results in a rocky rebound.

While tranquilizers are effective for acute symptom relief, they are actually counter-productive to long-term recovery. They instantly shut down the brain's ability to learn from experience. Research at the Stanford University School of Medicine in California, has also shown that tranquilizers don't prevent hyperarousal, but simply make us oblivious to it. (See Chapter 6.)

However, there is one pill I urge you to pop – a magnesium supplement! It won't just mask symptoms, but will naturally replenish your low reserves of mineral tranquillity and nourish your nerves at the root.

Magnesium – the original chill pill. The relaxation mineral. Magnesium is actually used in hospitals for seizures and heart failure. Less dramatically, it also helps with sleep. Our soils are depleted in magnesium, and consequently most of us are also depleted in this essential mineral that helps stabilize blood sugar. Magnesium is a natural muscle relaxant and a vital nutrient that is deficient in modern diets. Our ancient ancestors would have had a ready supply from organ meats, seafood, mineral water, and even swimming in the ocean, but things have changed – estimates put about 80% of people in developed countries in the "deficient" category, while recognizing that the remaining 20% are also very low.

Stress can contribute to magnesium deficiency, while a lack of magnesium tends to magnify the stress reaction – a typical vicious cycle. Magnesium deficiency is associated with systemic inflammation, while supplementation has been shown to suppress the ability of the hippocampus in the brain to stimulate the release of the stress hormone cortisol. Not only that, but it also reduces the release of ACTH, the hormone that tells your adrenal glands to get in gear and pump out cortisol and adrenaline. It also reduces the responsiveness of the adrenal glands to ACTH. And, as if that's not enough, magnesium can act at the blood brain barrier to prevent the entrance of stress hormones into the brain. What's not to like?

Studies have linked magnesium deficiency to anxiety and panic attacks, and I have met people who believe they resolved their anxiety with magnesium supplementation alone. Give it a go – even if it were to have no effect on your anxiety, you will definitely be doing your body a big favour. It is something instant and easy that you can do to help your nervous system – a perfect first practical step.

LET'S DO IT ♦ Fear-free Me

Witty banter abounds in the 2001 crime film *Heist*. At one point, Gene Hackman's character is asked how he devised such a convoluted caper. "I tried to imagine a fella smarter than myself," he says. "Then I tried to think, 'what would *he* do?'"

Take a few moments to imagine waking up tomorrow and feeling...

different. Feeling yourself to be at some higher vantage point, with a larger view and a newfound measure of calm and equanimity. You might even see yourself sitting above or next to your situation, rather than in it.

Imagine – suddenly the weight of the world has magically been lifted from your shoulders. All your old concerns have evaporated, even though the conditions of your life are still the same (money worries, interpersonal conflicts, looming deadlines), but you simply glide through each challenge.

You have never breathed so easy and felt so fresh – all the energy that has been entangled in fretting is now freed up.

What would you do on your first day of absolute freedom from fear? What would you do for the week or month ahead? Now that you are not afraid to take risks, how would you steer toward greater fulfilment?

Think and fantasize about this for some time. There are no right or wrong answers; the object is simply to reflect and familiarize yourself with your own fears and the role they play in your life – especially the unseen fears that keep you stuck.

You may discover that some fear does serve a useful purpose. But as you consider different scenarios and potentials in your life, ask yourself to what degree fears are really serving you, or holding you back.

Let your imagination run wild… then write it down. Putting pen to paper is important for this exercise, even just a few short notes.

We will come back to this exercise later. For now, let that image of yourself simply serve as a reference for self-discovery or insight. Dialogue with that alternate you. Ask what he or she has to say.

2

SWIMMING WITH SHARKS

As the city's dedicated shark spotters will attest, Danger Beach is ironically one of the safest swimming spots on Cape Town's notoriously infested coastline. While the submerged landscape creates perfect waves, it also keeps the sharks at bay. The regulars here know from experience why it's called Danger Beach – they've learnt to see below the surface, and can recognize the pull of the strong undercurrent that gives the lifeguards a daily run for their money.

The great mistake people make when they realize the rip has taken them, is to struggle. They panic and exhaust themselves, fighting to get back on solid ground in a hurry. And yet if they were able to keep calm and just tread water, they would be perfectly safe – further out, the current abates and you can wade back to shore a short distance down the beach. A person of average fitness could stay afloat for hours, yet most drownings happen in under five minutes.

Those who survive the battle, usually thanks to a surfer's help or a lucky wave, attest that drifting out over the deep is the distressing prospect that inspired their desperate struggle – once instinct kicks in, it overrides all good sense. Most people would rather exhaust themselves to the point of collapse than float out beyond the breaking waves among the unseen sharks.

And so it is the sharks after all – 99.9% imaginary – that makes Danger Beach so dangerous. The struggle is really a mental one.

The Prime Directive

Something significant happens when we enter the water. Within seconds, we plunge from the top of the food chain, right to the bottom. And that is when the part of the brain called the Sentinel really kicks into gear – the part that scans the environment for signs of anything fishy.

During our evolutionary history, the Sentinel would perk up any time we left our cave. In a world of lions, tigers and bears, our brains became brilliant at vigilance. Safety first and keep 'em peeled – survival is the prime directive.

Now that we are at the top of the food chain, you would think this vigilance would let up. But not so. Our culture is dog-eat-dog, and there is always a safer spot, a higher perch, a better position, and we must keep climbing. This has been our recipe for success as a species.

A big part of the Sentinel's job is prediction. Think for a few seconds about something you plan to do tomorrow. Chances are you saw a picture in your mind's eye. You have an idea of what tomorrow might look like, as if you saw into the future. This is really a unique feat, thanks to our brain's pre-frontal cortex – we are able to create alternate realities, to plot and plan and find the best strategic advantages and avoid potential pitfalls. Our brains are prediction-machines.

The problem is, they hardly *stop* creating alternate realities. For many of us, the off switch seems out of reach. The Sentinel doesn't just stand down when the coast is clear. It stays on the alert, scanning both the external and internal horizon for potential threats or disadvantages. It is an endless broadcast by the inner Department of Defence, analyzing old conflicts and plotting pre-emptive strikes with such relentless chatter that all we hear is Radio Gaga.

With every alternate reality, we create a subtle expectation. We are so good at this that most of the time we don't even know we are doing it. It's like an intravenous drip from the subliminal mind – every drop poses the question: *could this experience be better? Where's the advantage? Am I winning or losing?* We are so used to this process of evaluation, it mostly goes unseen and unquestioned. We are constantly comparing our given reality with a better fantasy. Our experience of life becomes imbued with a sense of lack; a constant, low-level dissatisfaction.

The Sentinel gives us what is called "negativity bias." This bias impels us to focus on what is wrong and ignore what does not need fixing. The glass is always half empty, because that is the problematic part. This is why we do not question the one-sided negativity in the daily news – good news is no news.

My garden is a more mundane example. Guests don't experience the same garden I do. They see the lawn and the colours of the flowers... I see the dead patch where the grass won't grow, the bushes that need trimming and the tangle of dead nasturtiums when spring has passed.

This process is so all-pervasive, it is mostly unconscious. We pay it no mind, but it taints our experience of life. This is why mindfulness-based Acceptance and Commitment Therapy (ACT) starts from the premise that the normal thinking processes of the healthy human brain will naturally lead to psychological suffering. The game of life is rigged, and not in our favour.

The good news is that we can change this state of affairs.

But first things first. We need to recognize the fundamental feeling that feeds this entire setup. What is the Sentinel's overriding emotion? On what is this unwavering vigilance based? What is the foundation of almost our entire experience?

Let's face it. We are all children of the Angel of Fear.

LET'S DO IT ♦ Jump Around

The most powerful feel-good strategy available to us is exercise. The parasympathetic (calming) nervous system is stronger in those who exercise, and numerous studies have shown exercise to be far more effective than antidepressants. It changes the brain, increasing the activity level of important brain chemicals such as dopamine and serotonin. It also increases the brain's production of a key growth hormone called BDNF. Because levels of this hormone plummet in depression, some parts of the brain start to shrink over time, and learning and memory are impaired. Exercise reverses this trend, protecting the brain in a way nothing else can. Physical effort also brings us back into our bodies, and helps halt the negative rumination for a while.

It is not *being* fit that makes you feel good, but simply *getting* fitter. Youth and perfect health are not necessary to feel the benefits – it is the physiological *process* of getting fit that makes the difference. How much exercise do you need? People say they take regular walks and consider it exercise. That might be valid after a certain age, but most of us need something more vigorous.

Balance is key. Too much *lactic acid* build-up from over-straining can increase anxiety! Many anxious people make this critical mistake after hearing about the benefits of exercise – they overdo it. If you overstrain, you cause a seesaw in your biochemistry, and what goes up, must come down. Marathon runners can get remarkably high during a race, but might find themselves in the doldrums the next day. If your nervous system is not sensitized, you may be able to get away with Olympic levels of exertion, but if you've been anxious, best drop the no-pain-no-gain attitude.

When exercising with the intention to heal, we have two good options. The first is garden-variety moderate, regular exercise. Moderate roughly means being able to *talk but not sing* while performing the exercise, and stopping while you still feel good, just before fatigue sets in. Activities as varied as hiking, biking, jogging, and weightlifting have all been found to be effective. Or try swimming, dancing or yoga (which balances the sympathetic and parasympathetic nervous systems).

The second option is a great time saver, and when you are stressed, the chances are that saving time is top of your list of priorities. It is called high-intensity interval training (HIIT). This involves pushing all out, but only for short bursts. This type of exercise has been scientifically shown to improve fitness and stamina more effectively than an hour on the treadmill. And it does this in only a fraction of the time. It will save you hours in the gym, and is the only exercise that naturally induces the release of the anti-ageing human growth hormone (HGH). It is also more effective at burning fat and building muscle. And it will only cost you between 4 to 8 minutes of physical exertion per week! Because you have to spend those few minutes at your maximum capacity, it is actually recommended not to do the exercise more than twice a week. Even once a week will show good improvements in fitness over time.

Whether it is healing the nervous system or investing your money, if some new strategy sounds too good to be true, it usually is. But HIIT is the exception. While I was still recovering from an over-sensitized nervous system, I chose more moderate aerobic exercise, but once I felt fully recovered, with my resilience tank topped up, I opted for an HIIT protocol called Peak 8. Peak 8 amounts to only 4 minutes of intense exercise per session. Done twice a week, that amounts to only 8 minutes of exertion per week! It doesn't really matter what type of aerobic exercise you are doing (I prefer skipping or sprinting on a beach).

Here is how it works: Use a stopwatch (available on most smartphones) and do 30 seconds of really intense cardio (skipping, running, cycling, but to your maximum capacity) and then take it easy for 90 seconds, shaking out, walking, stretching, catching your breath.

Then repeat that 8 times (amounting to 16 minutes in total). That's enough! If you have worked to your maximum capacity, you won't need to do more. In fact, in the beginning 8 repetitions may be too much – you can always start with 4 or 5 and increase the number as your fitness improves.

LET'S DO IT ♦ Recognize & Allow

Recognition and acceptance are the two crucial factors of mindfulness.

1. For one full minute, pause and ask yourself: What is happening inside me right now? Simply take a few moments to notice how you feel in your body. No need to label or analyze, just bring your awareness into your body. Concentrate on your *felt* experience. This is *recognition*.

2. Ask yourself: Can I allow this? Whatever it is you are feeling, whatever your inner experience is, even if unpleasant, give yourself permission to really allow it. See if you can temporarily forget about your intention to change or improve your present-moment experience. Let it be. As it is. This is *acceptance*.

3

TOOTH AND CLAW

Following the attack in the bay, the *Sunday Times* asked me to do a story about shark-researchers. I soon regretted accepting the assignment when, out in False Bay, a trillion tons of towering wave came roaring towards our boat. It was sunny and calm, but we were anchored off York Shoal, something our skipper had never tried before. And she would never be able to try it again: her research vessel was about to get sunk.

A manic scuttle erupted. Mariners clambered for cover. I jumpstarted and slipped in some shark bait that had been ladled overboard all morning. Sliding through this oily slick, I considered the odds of surviving a doggy paddle along the current of chum that ran towards Seal Island in the distance. Just my luck – I was about to splash my way through a stretch of water renowned for having the highest concentration of great white sharks in the world, basted in a substance designed to attract the interest of anything peckish within a three-mile radius.

I was sharply reminded of life's prime directive – *don't get eaten*. In seconds, my brain produced terrifying predictions in such profusion that what actually happened seemed almost unexpected – the monster wave collapsed on itself and boiled away beneath us, drenching us in spray.

The sea-hardy researchers had gone green around the gills, and joined in post-panic giggles with unconvincing bravado. As we weighed anchor and rumbled off to more placid waters while metabolizing adrenaline, I reflected – in the moment of crisis there had been a background part of me that seemed really calm. I recognized it only for being thrown into stark relief, in contrast to the fear and explosion of imagined outcomes.

The calm at the core of this experience was pure *awareness*. Void of judgment or comment, this part of me was simply observing. Many will attest to this experience during an accident – they find themselves clear, collected and capable during the event. Things happen too fast for appraisal. It is only afterward that the shock and trembling sets in. Bare awareness is a faculty that stands beyond fear.

Half an hour later, a great white shark, four metres from rudder to snout, was circling the boat. The chum had taken effect. In the time it chose to hang around, I caught something in its look, something more than mere fish. Something awake and ancient. It felt as if the real curiosity here was me – the fleeting evolutionary experiment.

I also realized that fear is primeval, hard-coded into biological existence, and as old as the food chain.

99 Percent of Human History

Sharks are apex predators, but this does not make them fearless. On the contrary, they can be quite skittish and circumspect. Their fight-or-flight response is far from off-line.

It is the same for us. Our nervous systems have evolved with the principle aim of avoiding jaws, yet we struggle to relax at the top of the food chain. The reason for this is simply that our nervous systems have evolved to deal very effectively with brief, short-lived stress – like evading a predator – but not with the constant low-level stress to which we subject ourselves in our complex civilization.

When a lion attacks, the crisis is acute. You can fight the feline, run like hell or climb a tree lickety-split. The options are limited and the outcome is decided in short order. The situation is acute, rather than chronic. When a springbuck escapes the clutches of death, it doesn't seem to suffer from post-traumatic stress, like one might expect. It has recourse to its natural de-traumatizing response, called neurogenic tremoring (see Chapter 9) because its nervous system, like ours, is so well adapted for acute, rather than chronic, scenarios.

In fact, the two types of stress could not be more different in their effect on us. Biologists confirm that acute stress is anabolic (makes us stronger), while chronic stress is catabolic (breaks us down). The low-level stress that is particular to our advanced culture may not feel as intense as evading a predator, but over time it wears us out. Piling relentless pressure onto neuronal hardware needs more than a two-week vacation once a year.

We need a strong sympathetic nervous system to be effective in the world. It is the accelerator we use to strive and achieve our goals. It is the biological basis for motivation. For peak performance, the accelerator relies on the parasympathetic nervous system, which is the brake. The two need to be in balance. In our post-industrial culture this part of the nervous system is neglected, which has resulted in an imbalance for which we are paying a steep price, not only in personal health, but also economically. This imbalance leads to a low-level burnout, to which we have become so accustomed we consider it normal.

Relaxation remains elusive unless we actively cultivate it and invest time and effort. It gets occasional lip-service, but mostly as a tool to further productivity. We do not relax so much as distract ourselves. Almost all our leisure activities are attempts to manage our moods – with varying but mostly limited degrees of long-term success. In our schools, meditation (what the father of modern psychology, William James, called *"the education par excellence"*) is still almost unheard of, while exercise is invariably competitive. Yoga? Nowhere in sight. (That said, there are a few pilot programmes around the world where mindfulness and yoga are now being introduced in schools, with encouraging results.) In the rush to rank ourselves, in search of praise and success and in service to Progress, relaxation has no place.

For 99.8% of human history, our lifestyles were those of hunter-gatherers. Contrary to the misapprehension that this lifestyle was "nasty, brutish and short," a revolution in archaeological thinking has come to consider the hunter-gatherer lifestyle as one of leisure and abundance. From the San people to the Hadza, the work of finding food took, on average, no more than three days out of every week, with the rest of the time mostly devoted to dancing, story-telling, games and ceremonial activities, with rich inner lives of spiritual journeying like vision quests, sweat lodges and walkabouts.

The myth of their much shorter life spans comes from statistical averaging – while their infant mortality was much higher than ours, they lived long lives in supportive, close-knit communities.

These are the conditions to which our nervous systems are suited – a far cry from the current state of affairs.

As the psychologist Erich Neumann has pointed out, the modern world is in "a crisis of fear." Evidence for this abounds, from the rising rates of depression and stress-related disorders, to the fact that technological advances, meant to save us time and afford us more leisure, has simply accelerated the speed with which we rush through our days and cram our sleep-deprived brains with information. The media regularly reports on "digital stress."

Advertising thrives on fear, cultivating catastrophobia and stimulating our desire for soothing consumption. TV ads for antibacterial soaps and chemical cleaning products encourage a fear of the invisible, while in the US, the advertising of psychotropic "medication" on television is off the scale. "Feeling a bit glum? We've got candy!" It's all pizza and antidepressants – and heaps of sugar to make the medicine go down. On *The Doctors* an antidepressant is recommended for premenstrual syndrome, while *New Scientist* reports on a study with a feature entitled *Television adverts for antidepressants cause anxiety*.

TV advertising is frequently interrupted by the news, and if you happen to be having dinner at the same time, indigestion is sure to follow. School shootings, sexual assault, global warming, corruption, terrorist bombings, drone strikes and their "collateral damage"... even if we don't experience accidents and atrocities first hand, violence is woven into the fabric of our lives and reverberates in our limbic brains with a constant hum. If you are not at least a bit scared, you simply *haven't been listening*.

Meanwhile parenthood becomes an ever-more fearful profession. Trutex, the leading school-uniform supplier in the UK, has recently started sewing tracking devices into their uniforms, while a study by the Children's Society found that 43% of parents in the UK believe their children should not be allowed out of the house until they are fourteen. (Interestingly, UK stats suggest that we would need to lock our children out of the home every day for 200 000 years before they would be abducted – and even then the chances are 85% that they would be found unharmed within 24 hours.)

Fear abounds. Yes, the world needs fixing, but so do we, and the quality of our solutions will reflect the clarity of our minds and hearts. Investing in ourselves and our inner wellbeing is no indulgence. It has the potential to change the world. Coming to terms with fear is the prime training for dealing with any difficulty.

LET'S DO IT ♦ Go Low GI

There is no way around it – to reduce stress and anxiety you must drastically decrease (preferably eliminate) sugar, breads and processed foods from your diet.

The connection between sugar and mental health has been studied for decades, and a tremendous amount has been written about its detrimental effect on people's physical and emotional wellbeing. And here is the key – blood-sugar fluctuations *within the normal range* will increase anxiety and stress. Testing your blood-sugar level at any given time is not all that significant, because it is rather *the rate* at which it rises and falls that affects your nerves.

Regular low blood sugar (hypoglycemia) is especially problematic. When your blood glucose drops, adrenaline and cortisol will be released to compensate, because adrenaline is needed to convert glycogen from the liver. To keep adrenaline down, keep your blood sugar stable. That does not mean constant grazing, or going full Banting (i.e. never eating any carbs, ever). It means eating healthy whole foods, enough protein and fat, and keeping the refined carbohydrates as low as possible. If you have a sweet tooth, replace the usual suspects with xylitol substitutes.

Starting the day with a protein breakfast (like free-range eggs) will reliably help to stabilize blood-sugar and hormone levels for the day ahead. As an alternative to high-GI carbohydrates in the evening, like potatoes, try mashed cauliflower. (Boil cauliflower, add feta and butter, and mash away. This is delicious – much better than it sounds!) Even grated cauliflower fried in a pan with plenty of organic or hormone- and antibiotic-free butter makes for a quick and healthy carb substitute.

Be sure to add some nutmeg. According to a study published in the *Journal of Medicinal Food*, an extract of nutmeg seeds elicited a significant antidepressant-like effect in mice; in some doses comparable in potency to some of the most powerful prescription antidepressants. In fact, reducing anxiety and treating insomnia are two ailments that nutmeg has been traditionally used for.

Fructose in fruit is also not a good idea, so when it comes to the old adage of five fruits and vegetables a day, rather make it seven vegetables daily and one fruit every few days. Protein and complex carbohydrates (i.e. vegetables) will help your over-strained pancreas heal itself and, along with regular exercise, reduce insulin resistance. If you need to wean yourself off bread, opt for sourdough rye bread, which qualifies as low-GI, or try grain-free crackers.

If persistent anxiety has been a problem, a few weeks of eating like this will make a remarkable difference and provide a solid foundation for healing. This is undoubtedly the diet for optimum resilience.

LET'S DO IT ♦ Rehydrate

Dehydration alone can cause anxiety. Low-level, constant dehydration undoubtedly contributes to stress, and some estimates suggest that up to 75% of people are chronically dehydrated.

When the body is dehydrated, blood flow slows down and the heart has to work harder. Hormones struggle to reach their destinations, and muscles tense up. The brain may experience weakness, dizziness or light-headedness as a result of water loss – the brain is 85% water.

Dr Batmanghelidj, a conventionally trained doctor and scientist, wrote *The Body's Many Cries for Water*. It got rave reviews in the press, and the *Journal of Clinical Gastroenterology* called it "a masterpiece." It describes how dehydration results in anxiety and exacerbates the stress cycle.

When we have elevated stress hormones in our body all the time, it forces fluids out of the system. We have runny tummies, we sweat. These things tend to dehydrate. Mother Nature has a mechanism for turning down our sense of thirst because She thinks there's a drought when we are dehydrated. The more dehydrated we get, the less thirsty we become, and the more dehydrated we get. A vicious circle.

When we have these powerful stress hormones in our system, the more dehydrated we become, the more concentrated and powerful those negative hormones coursing through our bloodstream become. As little as a 2% decrease in body water can lead to dehydration and performance detriments in sports. When your water levels decrease by higher levels like 3% or 4%, there are physiological changes that occur that may have health consequences, such as increased heart rate.

However, rehydration does not necessarily mean drinking more water. Beyond a certain point, that could dilute the digestive enzymes and upset the already fragile digestive process. To be properly hydrated, you need to replace fluid lost from the body with one that is similar to the body's natural composition. Watery fruit and vegetables often contain levels of minerals and sugar that mirror this, so they can hydrate you more effectively than water alone.

Some fruit and vegetables hydrate the body twice as effectively as a glass of water. Containing hydrating salts, minerals and sugars, they work in a similar way to the isotonic drinks favoured by athletes.

Top of the list is *watermelon*, which is 92% water, only 8% fructose, and contains essential rehydration salts calcium, magnesium, potassium and sodium.

Due to its 96% water content and mineral balance, a *cucumber* can produce similar hydration levels to twice the volume of water. It also contains almost ideal levels of calcium and magnesium, along with potassium, sodium and other minerals.

Two or three mineral-rich *celery* sticks replenish levels of sodium, potassium, magnesium, calcium, phosphorus, iron and zinc. These salts carry water around the body.

Some nutrition experts suggest that the ideal proportion of watery foods to concentrated foods should be 80% watery foods to 20% concentrated foods. Even if you were to narrow this margin considerably to 60% watery foods to 40% concentrated foods, it is still drastically different from many of our on-the-run diets. Hamburger and fries, pizza, or a sandwich – all of these are made up of mostly concentrated foods. Where does the body get the H_2O in these meals to create the digestive enzymes to break them down?

To know if you are drinking enough clean water, check that the colour of your urine is a very light yellow. Juicing also helps with hydration.

Drinking herbal tea is a great way to hydrate, and my favourite – tulsi – is good for increasing resilience. In Sanskrit, *tulsi* means "the incomparable one," and due to its use in religious ritual, came to be called *holy basil*. Agents that improve the body's ability to adapt to stressors are called adaptogens. In *Tulsi – The Mother Medicine of Nature*, Dr Narendra Singh studied an array of herbs, and found tulsi to be a vastly superior adaptogen that greatly boosts general stress resistance. Its chemical compounds also have strong anti-viral, anti-bacterial and immune-enhancing properties. It is a mild painkiller, helps reduce blood glucose levels, and reduces cholesterol.

Zen author and peace activist Thich Nhat Hanh suggests: "Drink your tea slowly and reverently, evenly, without rushing toward the future – as if it is the axis on which the earth revolves."

4

THE NATURE OF FEAR

If we are honest, we should be able to admit that there are sharks in swimming pools. Not always, and perhaps not in all pools. But sometimes, in a pool at night…

I might not have actually seen one, but there's no fooling me. I know they're there.

At least, a part of me seems to believe they could be. Otherwise why would I feel so skittish, splashing about in the dark with one eye cocked for a dorsal fin?

No cold logic changes the experience. And it does not have to be literal to be true. There are sharks in swimming pools.

Cognitive Contradiction

Irrational fears are tenacious and immune to statistical reassurance. For example, even though falling coconuts are more lethal than sharks, tropical beaches rarely induce morbid vigilance. Same with flying – many people go tight in the jaw during take-off in the full knowledge that they will technically be in much greater peril during the car ride home from the airport.

An argument that shows a particular fear to be irrational often fails to release its grip. As often as not, it does the opposite, adding a layer of consternation at the illogical waywardness of the mind.

There are two reasons for this. On the one hand, it's a matter of imagination. If an imagined calamity can be a dramatic scene in a movie, it holds greater sway over the mind. In other words, we fear the *filmic*. This is why slipping in the shower or choking on popcorn while watching TV does not have nearly the same charge as the prospect of hitting the tarmac in a conflagration of twisted metal as severed propellers saw into the flaming fuselage.

The point is, our imagination plays tricks. This is why horror movies work. Our imagination has an incredible capacity for suspension of disbelief.

Secondly, it is simply the way our brains are hard-wired.

The old limbic brain is where our emotions register. It is the part we have inherited from our early evolutionary ancestors. We can also call this the primal brain, as it is the seat of our primal impulses, prior to enculturation (good table manners).

Enveloping the primal brain is the mammalian cerebral cortex. The frontal lobes are what make us human – basically the *sapiens* part of *homo sapiens*. The cerebral cortex gives us the capacity for rational thinking and conceptualization, while the frontal cortex is the seat of self-awareness and impulse control.

Neuroscientists speak about the cerebral cortex and the limbic system as two separate brains. So here is the crucial part: when it comes to the irrational nature of fear, *the neuronal synapses leading from the rational brain to the primal brain are few and far between compared to the synapses leading the other way.* In short: the primal brain has the upper hand.

And that is why, when an emotion has us in its grip, it is so difficult to switch it off or just talk ourselves out of it, even if we can recognize that we are over-reacting out of all sensible proportion. We assume that we should be able to think our way out of fear, but when it comes to controlling our emotions, the neurological cards are stacked against us.

In an informal experiment, Darwin demonstrated this to himself while writing *The Expression of the Emotions in Man and Animals*. He visited the puff adder enclosure at the London Zoo, determined to keep his nose pressed to the glass each time the snake would strike, in the safe certainty that the pane was far too thick to crack, much less break. But each time the snake lashed out, he couldn't stop himself from pulling away, putting a gap between nose and glass. The primal brain – with its amygdala where fear and anxiety register – has a certain dominance over the conceptual brain. In potent situations, instinct trumps reason.

In light of this, the paradoxical approach of acceptance actually becomes sensible. When the primal mind is activated and in the grip of fear, our attempts at control are an uphill battle, simply adding stress to stress.

Many books and professionals promise to help us overcome and get rid of fear, stress and anxiety. "You must get on top of this thing," I was told many times. "Don't let it get the better of you. Don't let it go on too long. Get help. Be careful. Watch out." Behind these fearful and fighting words lurks the vague implication: *or else*. Whether through positive affirmations or the chemical cosh, they exhort us to conquer.

And so we wrestle the angel, while the angel patiently awaits our surrender.

REVERB

The words stress, fear and anxiety all denote activation of what is called the HPA-axis – the hypothalamus, pituitary and adrenal glands. One could say that, biologically, it is all roughly the same thing. And yet anxiety is particularly interesting, because it is an amplification of irrational fear.

Anxiety is feeling afraid when there is nothing obvious to fear. It seems to arise out of nowhere... but in fact it is conditioned, secretly fuelled by subliminal storylines and fantasies that undermine an already over-sensitized nervous system. In this way it is both physical and mental.

The body and mind function in synergy. Like the yin-yang symbol, the one affects and contains the other, echoing back and forth. The rapidity of this echoing effect makes diagnostic discernment almost redundant, and makes causes a lot less relevant than we have been led to believe. Is the fear physical or psychological? We can safely trust that it's both.

Nervous-system sensitization is no mystery, we have all felt it. Getting cut off in rush-hour traffic after a difficult day at work, only to find the dog has dug up all the flower beds you spent the weekend planting... Your partner had better watch out, because you are on the edge, and a few badly chosen words will make you go Krakatoa. That is sensitization.

When chronic sensitization starts to appear as physical symptoms like cold sweats, nausea or heart palpitations, we become bewildered. The stranger the symptoms, the stronger the bewilderment, and believe me, the symptoms of over-sensitization can become weird indeed. Body zaps, crawling sensations on the skin, feelings of unreality, headaches... you name it – for the nervous system there is no business like show business. A regular house of horrors, and yet these symptoms are invariably false alarms.

The smallest and most trivial things can set us off. If this continues for some time, we cannot help but compare the present with the past. *We never used to be like this.* One feels changed in some deep and dangerous way, becoming afraid of one's own condition. Worrying about it, trying to fight or run – the fight-or-flight response.

And so, adding stress to stress, fear to fear.

The problem is that first fear – the unseen fear; fear of more fear; fear of an escalation of fear that is overwhelming. An angry wave. Full and final annihilation.

This first fear is present for everyone, whether the anxiety seems "pathological" or not. Not only do we fear the proverbial lions, tigers and bears, but we fear the fear, spending time and effort placating this unseen fear. It may seem dormant, or feel simply like worry, and we may think it only occasional, but make no mistake: it is powerful and pervasive, and we are its slaves.

Anxiety is a feedback loop. Fundamentally, it is the fear of fear. Reverb. An ouroboros – the snake swallowing its own tail.

Here Be Monsters

The mind spins predictions and simulates conflicts to a degree that is wholly unnecessary. Many people complain of feeling drained and exhausted – like playing high-stakes chess non-stop. With this mental activity we create our own stress.

Mark Twain said: "I am an old man and have known a great many troubles, but most of them never happened." Of course, real calamities are stressful, but stress is not something that happens *to* us. When you begin to practise sitting mindfulness, you soon notice how runaway thoughts constantly recreate tension in the body, and how hopping off that train of thought renews the relaxation.

So with the Sentinel at the helm, watching out for number one, we constantly amplify stress. This egocentric Sentinel is fundamentally fuelled by fear.

Fear, therefore, is the root cause of stress.

I have found that executives seldom confess to feeling fear when I teach mindfulness in corporate environments, and yet they will readily admit to being stressed. *It is the same thing* – most modern-day chronic stress is rooted in fear.

Exam stress is simply fear of failure. Performance anxiety is fear of humiliation. Nervous to ask someone on a date? It is because you fear they will say no. Stressed because you cannot answer all your emails? Afraid of what other people will think or say if they don't get a prompt response?

Are you one of the working wounded, with too much on your plate? Not enough time in the day? The question becomes: what is the fear behind ignoring your limits? What are you trying to measure up to; who are you trying to impress? And what is the fear if you don't?

This all amounts to a remarkable irony – while fear functions to keep us alive, it is also what is eventually most likely to kill us. Research continually confirms that stress is the greatest cause of heart disease, the number one killer in the world. (The maligned egg, it would seem, is innocent of mass murder – see two books that share the title *The Great Cholesterol Con* by Anthony Culpo and by Malcolm Kendrick respectively.) When the poet Emerson said, "Fear defeats more people than any other one thing in the world," he was more literally right than he knew.

The function of fear is avoidance. *Here be monsters* – right, let's not sail there then. It is based on what *could* happen, and starts with *what if*. What if I never recover? What if this country goes to the dogs? What if the test comes back positive? Fear suspends disbelief and gears up for some serious avoidance.

In this way fear is future-based. One could say "fear" is an acronym for "future expectations assumed real." The bare-bones storyline of fear is always: I can handle *this* moment, but I am not so sure about the next. A minute from now, I may lose control. Tonight I will be expected to sit still and relax... what if I can't? This feels awful... what if it is still with me in the future?

The imagined calamity is always a step or ten ahead of us. In other words, it is a fantasy. More accurately, a fantasy resisted. *Fear is resistance to a fantasy.* So, we can recognize it as rather empty. A paper tiger, a shadow play. Incorporeal. Almost like – an angel perhaps?

Because its very nature is resistance, our natural urge is to wrestle, struggle and fight... and in so doing we mistake it for a demon. The challenge is to entertain the question: Could personal demons be angels in disguise?

To do this we must learn to relax our resistance. As Jung noted: "What you resist will persist." The way of mindfulness is to cultivate our capacity to allow. This attitude of acceptance is all-encompassing – when we feel fear, we will feel resistance, and we allow this too.

Jung observed that his patients who achieved a sense of liberation and integration, and deeper levels of psychological development, essentially did nothing but *allow things to happen*.

> "The art of letting things happen, action through inaction, letting go of oneself as told by Meister Eckhart, became for me the key that opens the door to the way. We must be able to let things happen in the psyche. For us, this is an art of which most people know nothing. Consciousness is forever interfering, helping, correcting, and negating, never leaving the psychic process to grow in peace."

Or as Voltaire summed it up: "The art of medicine consists in amusing the patient while Nature effects the cure."

This inner movement toward acceptance is the great key, but it is not just a switch you flip in your mind and suddenly everything is coming up roses. It is a slow and gradual inner training as we shift our attitude, ever more toward unconditional acceptance of our inner environment.

LET'S DO IT ♦ Six Steps to ACCEPT

It is rarely easy to accept when an emotional storm is whipping through our minds and bodies. This process breaks acceptance down into manageable steps.

A – Acknowledge

Simply acknowledge the difficulty and name it. Acknowledge also your resistance to the feeling. Often we try to deny or suppress what we are feeling. The first step is to face the simple fact of what is happening. For example: *I am feeling scared, and it feels as if my thoughts are racing.* Or: *I feel overwhelmed and exhausted.* Whatever it is, just stop for a moment to feel what you are feeling, rather than trying to ignore or suppress it.

C – Consider
Consider the nature of the feeling. Investigate it with some questions, like: Where is it felt in the body? Is there any tensing around it? Does it feel solid or permanent? What associations come up in your mind around this feeling? Are you stressing yourself with "what if" questions, letting catastrophic thoughts or exaggerated scenarios carry you away? No need to get entangled in an analysis – the task here is simply to notice.

C – Care
Care about yourself enough to bring self-compassion to the situation. First see, and then let go of any judgments. If you think you deserve to feel this, that is a judgment. If you think you should not be feeling this, or that you should be stronger, that is also a judgment. Whatever you are feeling, it is not your fault. It is simply part of the human condition. Ask yourself: "If someone I really loved was confronted with this feeling or experience, how would I treat them in the kindest and most caring way? What might I say or do?" Apply to yourself your answers to these questions.

E – Embrace
This is the crucial step, and it may require a bit of courage. Embrace all your feelings, even if just for one minute. Allow yourself to feel them just as they are. This can sometimes be done with the breath – breathe into wherever the difficulty is felt in the body. This does not mean you fuse with the feelings – instead you just become the impartial space for them to express themselves. Then welcome any feelings behind feelings – behind fear there is sometimes distress, sadness, grief, confusion or even anger. Embrace them all by allowing them to be felt on their own terms, without preconceived notions.

P – Pursue your values
Pursue a course of action in line with your values. Ask yourself: "In the face of this difficulty, what do I want to stand for? How can I act in a way that I will be proud of when I look back on this?" It does not need to be a grand gesture; it can be a tiny step in the right direction, like going for a short jog or simply relaxing the tension in your body. Then ask yourself what you could do in the next hour or two that would resonate with your sense of goodness, truth or beauty. Commit to a meaningful course of action, rather than an addictive or habitual strategy to try to get rid of the feeling. Aim to respond in a constructive way.

T – Trust

Finally, trust that uncomfortable feelings will pass in their own time. This is guaranteed. No feeling is final.

LET'S DO IT ♦ The Gratitude Attitude

One of the best practices to counteract our natural negativity bias, or the Sentinel's view of the world, is to keep a basic gratitude journal. Studies have corroborated its far-reaching beneficial effects, especially on stress by improving heart-rate variability. It may seem like a pointless gesture, but it has a cumulative effect that far outweighs the tiny effort. In time, this will also prompt you to recognize life's daily richness.

Try this thirty-day gratitude exercise and see for yourself – it is as effective as it is simple. Every night before bed, jot down five things from that day for which you are grateful. They do not have to be big things. It could be a kind comment, a smile, a cathartic cry, a butterfly or the way the sun reflected off a puddle. Anything. The challenge is never to repeat the same thing. Each day has its own experiences.

This does not have to be kept. Even a scrap of paper will do. The value lies in the *doing*. Your mind is being trained to recognize the goodness and beauty that already surround you.

PART 2: KEYS TO ACCEPTANCE

5

GROUND CONTROL

In 1953, US Air Force test pilot Chuck Yeager – the first person to fly faster than the speed of sound – was breaking another record high above the Nevada desert when his aircraft started pitching, rolling and yawing out of the sky.

The cockpit erupted in advice from the tower, but the prognosis was not good – when things went *this* wrong, the result was always a crater. At extreme altitudes the laws of aerodynamics drop away, and even with the world's most skilled pilots applying correction after correction, standard navigation strategies invariably proved pointless.

This time, however, the pilot failed to follow the frenzied advice. In the violence of the plane's tumbling, Yeager had lost consciousness. For a full minute the jet hurtled toward earth. And then, re-entering the denser atmosphere, it began to stabilize by itself. When Yeager came to, he was able to guide the craft to a safe landing.

It became clear that the scramble for control was not the solution. In fact, it was counter-productive At a certain point, the best strategy was no strategy at all – simply let go of the controls.

The Happiness Trap

Being tossed end over end at Mach 2 is what it can feel like when you are in panic. Curbing the instinct to regain control can require a supreme measure of faith. Not so much the faith that everything *will be* all right, but rather that the intensity *is* all right.

This level of acceptance of the present moment in extremis is both radical and counter-intuitive. It is what the Buddha called *patisotagami* – "going against the stream" of our conditioned reflexes and habits.

When we find ourselves in full flight with anxiety, or in disorienting freefall, letting go of the controls and doing nothing – applying acceptance – is likely to feel reckless and irresponsible. This is understandable. After all, your entire distributed nervous system is telling you to fight or run – essentially, to *do something* about the situation. Faith may fail us.

Yet we can recognise that our lack of faith is also culturally conditioned. "Culture is your operating system," and society functions on certain sets of assumptions, which we internalize. It may help to question some of these assumptions.

The first common misconception is that *happiness is the natural default state for human beings.*

We assume this because it is what we see. In our media we see smiles and glamour on the red carpet, and beaming joy in ads for shampoo and toothpaste. In most movies, protagonists ride into the sunset happily ever after. Unlike the news, these are the people or characters with whom we identify emotionally.

Those we meet in life also seem to be totally on top of things, and we forget that all we see is their personas – the polished facades, not the full personality with its inner conflicts and self-doubt. We compare our inner realities to their outer masks, exposing ourselves to the recurring suspicion that we do not quite measure up.

Attending many intensive retreats designed to take participants to the edge and unpack their inner wounds, I have witnessed how the behaviour of the person you meet on day one during chit chat is mostly a performance. By day four everyone has had their chance to fall apart amid trembling and tears. From lawyers and businessmen to artists and psychologists… at some point the persona gives up the act and the mask is dropped.

It is remarkable how many people are crying – just not visibly. As children growing up, we do not learn to stop crying so much as hide it. "Be kind, for everyone you meet is fighting a hard battle," said Plato.

The implication of this misconception is that, if we are not happy, there must be something wrong with us. You can test this. The next time someone asks how you are, reply: "I feel awful, thanks for asking." They will immediately show (or at least feign) grave concern and ask why. Nonchalantly answer: "Don't know." Then stand back and watch them try to solve your crisis.

Western society assumes that mental suffering is abnormal, indicative of a defect. It is seen as an illness in need of a cure, or a weakness. And yet, statistically the chance that you will suffer from a "psychiatric disorder" at some point in your life is about 30%. And that is not counting all the misery that does not classify as "psychiatric" – divorce, work stress, midlife crisis, illness, old age, shame or social isolation…

It speaks to the ubiquity of this assumption that, after his enlightenment, the first thing the Buddha pointed out, was that life is hard. His first teaching was that life is "dukkha" (the Pali word can be translated as "stress"). The etymology of the word refers to a broken or uneven axle under a horse-drawn cart, implying that the ride is not as comfortable as advertised.

The second common cultural assumption is that *we must get rid of negative thoughts and feelings if we want to be happy.*

The premise in "positive thinking" is that if we banish negativity and fill our minds with only positive thoughts and affirmations, we will become happier. It promises the world, but its effect is cosmetic.

The single-minded pursuit of the positive and pleasant is not genuinely transformative, but rather tends to get us stuck in a narrow passage that rejects the full range of human experience. In favouring only one side of the spectrum of our inner lives, we struggle to suppress everything that does not conform to our preferred state of mind. This is exhausting and creates deep tension. It puts a proverbial elephant in the room, by amplifying our personal "shadow."

The shadow is a Jungian term referring to all the unwanted, judged and rejected aspects of ourselves that we seek to deny the existence of and give expression to. But because these parts are only natural (and from some perspectives potentially positive), they do not go away, but rather coagulate in the unconscious.

Embarrassingly, this is blinding ourselves. We refuse to see our own suppressed traits and aspects… but most other people can! The tactful honesty of family, friends or skilful therapists becomes invaluable, provided their well-intentioned reflections do not topple us into critical self-judgment, which only compounds the problem. When the flavour of criticism creeps into therapy, it is counter-productive. Because we will let Hitler off the hook before we stop attacking ourselves.

Another simple way to acknowledge these parts of ourselves is to make a list of other people's characteristics that annoy us. Ask yourself: what really pushes my buttons? Perhaps not every item on that list will be part of your shadow material, but many will, and coming to compassionate terms with these aspects of ourselves is the way toward psychological wholeness.

Without this movement toward wholeness through integration, or what Jung called "individuation," we are split off from valuable and sometimes powerful parts of ourselves. We are fractured and cling to a constricted sense of self, often constructed quite arbitrarily. It may even show itself in a sense of isolation. This is the real imbalance we should focus on – a certain one-sidedness that Jung recognized as characteristic of neurosis:

> "I have frequently seen people become neurotic when they content themselves with inadequate or wrong answers to the questions of life. They seek position, marriage, reputation, outward success of money, and remain unhappy and neurotic even when they have attained what they were seeking. Such people are usually confined within too narrow a spiritual horizon. Their life has not sufficient content, sufficient meaning. If they are enabled to develop into more spacious personalities, the neurosis generally disappears."

The injunction to get rid of negative thoughts and feelings, with its preference for only the positive, creates a one-sided imbalance that actually *increases* neurosis. Yet it is still strongly promoted by a certain self-help contingent. I have personally encountered people who claim that their severe anxiety was initially kindled by the popular book and film *The Secret*. Everything must be love and light, and if you think only good thoughts, good things will "manifest." This contrived mental intervention makes us guarded, lest we spoil the drinking water or make ourselves sick. It mistakes sanitation for spirituality, and finds moral superiority in wish fulfilment. In short, what it calls "beyond rationality," is rather beneath it.

This exclusive orientation toward the positive also diminishes our capacity for discomfort – a capacity we surely need in spades when pursuing meaningful endeavours, like starting a business or a relationship, or having a child. But this assumption is not all our own fault. A feel-good society tends to favour pleasant experiences and neglect meaningful depth, richness and subtlety. As philosopher Ken Wilber writes:

> "It is often said that in today's world, the forces of darkness are upon us. But I think not; in the Dark and the Deep there are truths that can always heal. It is not the forces of darkness but of shallowness that everywhere threaten the true, and the good, and the beautiful, and that ironically announce themselves as deep and profound. It is an exuberant and fearless shallowness that everywhere is the modern danger ... and that everywhere nonetheless calls to us as saviour.
>
> We might have lost the Light and the Height; but more frightening, we have lost the Mystery and the Deep, the Emptiness and the Abyss, and lost it in a world dedicated to surfaces and shadows, exteriors and shells, whose prophets lovingly exhort us to dive into the shallow end of the pool head first."

The move to rid ourselves of negative inner content implies that we should be able to control our thoughts and feelings in the first place – and yet these control issues are conditioned. How often have we heard: *Stop crying, stop feeling sorry for yourself. You're overreacting. Get over it. Don't be a chicken. Snap out of it.* Such phrases imply that we should be able to control our feelings, a message reinforced by adults while we were growing up. Meanwhile the adults were developing stomach ulcers, having affairs, drinking too much, taking tranquilizers, and losing their tempers. Because, as already shown, we have a lot less control over our primal brain than we would like to admit.

These two cultural assumptions – that happiness should be our default setting, and that we can achieve this through getting rid of negative thoughts – set us up for a life-long struggle. This is a trap. Stop struggling and escape the trap!

We have seen that a mind left to its own devices is inclined toward a certain "negativity bias." Described above is what I call a "positivity bias." While it seeks to counterbalance our natural negativity, a bias is always unbalanced, and two wrongs do not make a right. It is like trying to put a car in reverse while going full speed down the highway – all you do is strip the gears.

The mindful solution is to come to neutral and let the momentum wear itself out. In other words, "let go of the controls."

LET'S DO IT ♦ Befriend the Fear

When struggling with the angel, it is tempting to try to run away. But running is even more futile than resistance. However fast or far we flee, the angel has wings, and demands to be faced.

It is difficult to allow or accept distress or discomfort when these feelings are fed by unacknowledged fears. When a fear remains vague, it moves in the shadows, evading exposure. Our first task is to face, expose and explore our fears, before letting them be.

As we uncover our fears, it is helpful to keep asking: what is the fear behind the fear? In this way we can get to the emotional core.

The following six-step journaling process has proven very powerful for me and my workshop participants.

1. Find the fear

To befriend your fear, you first have to find it. Ask yourself: *what is the fear that is feeding this stress I'm feeling right now?*

It might even be a minor fear, but it will disturb the mind if it remains unseen, and block your ability to come into a calmer, present-moment awareness. The stress you may be feeling right now, is an emotional distress. See if you can, just for a moment, allow the distress, and actually *feel* it… then see if you can tell what the fearful storyline is behind it.

Let's take a stressful traffic scenario. Perhaps you are afraid that if you get home twenty minutes later than planned, you won't be able to spend enough time with your children before they have to go to bed.

Can you do anything about what is causing the stress? If so, do it. If not, recognize that it is out of your control, and keep moving toward inner acceptance with the following steps.

2. What is behind the fear?

What is the worst that could happen? Keep asking this until you recognize the emotional core. To use our example above: Do you fear being a bad parent? Do you fear someone will point the finger and judge you for being neglectful or inadequate? Are you afraid your children are desperate for your presence? Or perhaps you have things you want to do when you get home, like take the dogs for a walk or jog before it gets dark. What is the fear behind that? Are you afraid you might be living a life that is somehow *unlived?* That does not allow you enough time to invest in yourself and your meaningful interests?

The aim here is not to fix the fears, but to befriend them. It requires focus on your inner environment. Take time to go down the rabbit hole and find the fears digging away down there.

3. Ask: is this true?
Often the fear is seen to be unfounded when exposed, and little more than a fantasy. If this is the case, recognize it. The very fact that you fear being a bad parent, makes you a pretty good parent already.

Either way, move on to the next step.

4. Accept the fearful situation
This is the crucial step: imagine that this fear comes true, that it has happened. If you have identified a core fear, try to get cosy with it. You have been suppressing it for long enough, and that has sapped your energy. Now look the imagined catastrophe full in the face, and meet it with as much acceptance as you can. Watch your attitude as you do this. There will be the habitual resistance, but the trick is to play with the feeling of acceptance, and see if you can be the space for the fear. Then from that space, you now formulate a clear, basic plan of action.

5. Plan for action
Assuming your fear has come true, what can you actually do about it to deal with the situation? Who do you need to call or speak to? What is your plan B? How will you compensate, or move forward in a meaningful way?

Decide on a concrete contingency plan. Do not indulge in rumination. *Write this down.* Once the plan of action is put down on paper, and you know what your next steps will be, it will stop haunting you and feeding your stress. You will know what to do, and will not have to compose an elegant response while you are discomposed.

6. Let go
Finally, let go of the fear and the plan. If the situation was out of your control, and you have developed a worst-case contingency plan, you have really done all you can do. It is out of your hands now, you can let go. If the fear is still there, that's fine, but let it sit in the passenger seat as you refocus on a meaningful way forward with your day – it has had its chance to speak and be heard.

The more you can practise befriending your fears, ideally followed by a brief mindfulness practice, you will begin to find yourself a lot less stressed in general.

6

PARADIGM SHIFT

Dressed to the nines, patrons arrived at the Théâtre des Champs-Élysées in Paris on a warm May evening in 1913. Nobody could have predicted that the music and choreography of the ballet they came to enjoy would incite a full-blown riot.

Until the curtain rose for the first time on Igor Stravinsky's *Rite of Spring*, ballet had been elegance and charm – *Swan Lake* and *Sleeping Beauty*. Now suddenly people were confronted with pagan fertility rites and a ritual of sacrifice in which a young girl dances herself to death. The score was adventurous, to put it mildly. The intense, primitive rhythms and use of dissonance caused catcalls and booing. As the protest gained momentum, arguments erupted between supporters and those offended by the work. Fistfights broke out in the aisles. The unrest degenerated into a riot. At intermission the Paris police arrived to restore order, but the second half of the performance once again turned into total chaos.

Stravinsky himself became enraged and ran backstage where the impresario was turning the lights on and off in a misguided attempt to calm the audience. The brawling and booing was so loud the dancers struggled to hear the orchestra, so Nijinsky, the choreographer, was leaning out from a chair to shout counts for them to keep the rhythm, with Stravinsky hanging onto his coat-tails to prevent him from falling over.

The composer had pioneered such a radical evolution for Western music that it caused bedlam in an audience that thought of itself as "civilized." The composer Puccini would call it "the work of a madman." "I had only my ear to help me," said Stravinsky. "I heard it and I wrote what I heard. I am the vessel through which *The Rite* passed."

The hysteria could have implied failure, but for Stravinsky it confirmed the work's transformative potency. A year later, after another performance, he would find himself carried through the streets on the shoulders of a cheering crowd. Today *The Rite of Spring* is considered a milestone in the history of music, inspiring countless composers and even influencing John Williams's score for the film *Star Wars*.

CHAOS IS GOOD

"Chaotic situations must not be rejected," wrote Chögyam Trungpa, one of the foremost figures in Tibetan Buddhism's transmission to the West. "Nor must we regard them as regressive, as a return to confusion. We must respect whatever happens to our state of mind. Chaos should be regarded as extremely good news."

As with the first performance of *The Rite*, chaos spells transformation. Crisis and consternation are its calling cards. Precisely because the time has come to fall apart, the psyche in chaos feels like it is going to pieces. Confusion reigns as the old orientations are lost. Kali is in the house.

Transformation causes fear. We prefer the familiar, the status quo, even though our souls may be weary of the current sources of refuge – our comfort zones. No wonder we become symptomatic... perhaps an angel is trying to grab our attention because we haven't been attuned to the subtle cues. "To see the angel in the malady requires an eye for the invisible," wrote the great psychologist James Hillman.

Before butterflies are born, worms work compulsively to cocoon themselves in a self-protective insulation. Perhaps their instinct is defensive, their metamorphosis feeling at first like impending annihilation... You may have been growing, but the confines of your world have now become as narrow as a coffin. It is constricting and claustrophobic. But consciousness obstructs its own evolution for fear of death. Reluctantly the mind is called upon to expand, but because that requires dropping its moorings it rarely wants to. With the concomitant fear of becoming "unhinged," and casting off, naturally this feels scary. Rather the cocoon we know than the unfathomable cosmos.

At the start of metamorphosis, the immediate future seems filled with mortal destruction. When the time has come for consciousness to evolve, the friction of our resistance to transform will cause anxiety. (Remember, in the exterior, material domain, it is simply a sensitized nervous system due to chronic stress. But that does not negate deeper significance in the interior, subjective domain of soul or spirit.)

In pagan, shamanic or traditional cultures, an encounter with fear plays a crucial part in initiation ceremonies, while a chaotic illness is often considered an "initiation sickness," heralding the eventual dawning of a new purpose (and altered world view). Even if we would like to, this process cannot be rushed. Usually the best we can do is simply learn to trust the natural unfolding. An attitude of acceptance is the precondition for letting go.

"When I let go of what I am, I become what I might be," says the *Tao Te Ching*.

In the previous chapter we looked at our tendencies to control our inner environment. The usual tactics are suppression, denial, or frantic distraction; even the more pro-active approach of positive thinking. These strategies are counter-productive.

But there is arguably an even greater deterrent to inner development. One of the most powerful impediments to acceptance is the materialist medical paradigm and its propaganda of "chemical imbalance."

BALANCING ACT

Following the Frenchman Philippe Petit's "artistic crime of the century" – the wondrous high-wire walk in 1974 between the twin towers of the World Trade Center in New York City – the imaginative daredevil was arrested and subjected to psychiatric examination.

As an eccentric figure, Petit seemed destined to fall under the scrutiny of modern psychiatry, which prefers to see humans conform to their notion of normal. Petit disregards societal rules and regulations, and tolerates an unusual degree of mortal danger. In an interview, he would later say: "I think when you describe people you are making a mistake. That's not how they are, that's how you perceive them at that moment. It's limiting in front of something that is magnificent and unlimited: life. To put the mind in a box is a crime. I see kids who go to psychiatrists, and I think, my God, what is happening?"

Petit was referring to the excessive use of psychiatry, which in turn has prompted an ever-growing anti-psychiatry movement, peopled not only by former "patients" but by many trained in psychiatry.

One of the earliest and most vocal in the anti-psychiatry movement was Dr Thomas Szasz, whose opposition started in 1961 with *The Myth of Mental Illness*. Szasz received several honorary degrees and awards, but predictably his consistent challenges to institutional psychiatry drew strong criticism from the psychiatric fraternity, as well as attempts to limit his academic freedom.

Fifty years after the publication of his seminal work, Szasz wrote: "My great, unforgivable sin in *The Myth of Mental Illness* was calling public attention to the linguistic pretensions of psychiatry and its pre-emptive rhetoric." This sentiment has been seconded by the respected psychologist James Hillman, who said: "Above all else, I distrust the language of psychopathology."[1]

In his scathing critiques of the medical paradigm of psychiatry, Szasz not only argued for an alternative paradigm, but explicitly sought to show that psychiatry was a "pseudoscience." In 1989, Karl Menninger, the long-time patriarch of American psychiatry, wrote to Szasz: "I think I understand better what has disturbed you these years and, in fact, it disturbs me, too, now."

This doubting Thomas paved the way for many to follow, like Dr Allen Frances, who spearheaded the anti-*DSM-5* movement and wrote the wonderfully titled *Saving Normal: An Insider's Revolt Against Out of Control Psychiatric Diagnosis, DSM-5, Big Pharma and the Medicalization of Ordinary Life*. The irony is that Dr Frances had actually led the task force that produced the previous edition of the *Diagnostic and Statistical Manual of Mental Disorders (DSM)*!

Psychiatrists routinely use the *DSM* to diagnose "disorders" and write prescriptions for psychotropic drugs (or what Szasz cannily called the "chemical cosh"), and Dr Frances came to believe that it has contributed to the rocketing rates of bogus mental illnesses. He says: "What motivates me is the experience of having inadvertently contributed to fads and psycho-diagnosis that have resulted in over-diagnosis and over-treatment..." While he recognizes that much of the problem was already prevalent in the *DSM-4*, he characterizes the many changes to the *DSM-5* as "unsupported and, in some cases, quite reckless."

Indeed, the criteria for diagnosis has expanded exponentially, and an alarming array of human experiences now masquerade as maladies, for which there is invariably a drug available. For example, if you have spent six months or more thinking about your medical issues, you may have Somatic Symptom Disorder, which seems like the perfect catch-all. If

---

[1] *The Myth of Analysis*, Northwestern University Press, 1973

you tend to hypochondria, you will happily agree: "Ooo yes, I have that!" It applies to almost anyone with irritable bowels or chronic pain.

There is also something quite mechanized about the *DSM-5*'s assessments on what constitutes normal or appropriate bereavement, and when the grief over the loss of a loved one should be considered Persistent Complex Bereavement Disorder. But then it is perfectly appropriate coding for a culture whose scientific materialism tends to see humans as little more than biological robots, and regards consciousness as a deluded product of the brain. While I do not doubt that, individually, psychiatrists genuinely wish to help, it is this reductionist paradigm that is also driving the mass drugging of children, which is widely considered to have reached tragic proportions.

The objection here is that labelling extreme or intense human emotions, even persistent ones, as psychiatric "disorders" is clearly not conducive to a culture of acceptance. The famous psychiatrist Stanislav Grof has spent a lifetime arguing that pathologies are signposts for what he coined "spiritual emergence."

While chemical intervention should always be a last resort, it has become very much the first resort. This sadly serves to make radical acceptance feel reckless and irresponsible.

Cocktails, Anyone?

Should you try medication for your anxiety or panic? If you are super sharp, you can guess my sentiments on the matter. But that does not mean I am not sympathetic to the impulse. On the contrary, it was an option I tried myself.

Getting a prescription was easy, if expensive. I was encouraged to take a full dose of the latest antidepressant. That afternoon, I took half. That night, I lay awake, grinding my teeth, my heart crawling up my gullet. By morning, when I staggered outside, all signs of the zombie apocalypse was miraculously gone, but my eyesight would only come back into proper focus by lunchtime.

Admittedly my negative reaction to the drug was extreme, but I know people who have had similar reactions, and whose psychiatrists disarmingly encouraged them to persist through the "side effects" until they passed, as the brain goes through a series of compensatory adaptations to the drug.

I was not made of such stern stuff, so when this last resort failed, I did not bother to ask whether a different drug might be the ticket.

I had simply run out of options. I sat at my kitchen table and had a short cry. There was no way out anymore, so I finally gave up.

And that was the beginning of my recovery.

I have since met several people who insist that antidepressants saved their lives. Who am I to argue? We do what we must. If it had worked for me, I might be saying the same thing today. I cannot help but suspect, though, that I would still be burdened by the same perspectives, the same habits, the same certainties and mental orientations – the same consciousness.

There is a scientific view that supports my suspicion that it would have been a case of arrested development. The rising rates of mental illness, in lock step with the growth of psychiatry, has prompted independent researchers to a more rigorous analysis. This revealed that long-term reliance on antidepressants is correlated with much higher relapse rates.[2] In other words, restoring "chemical balance" simply does not get at the root of the problem. This confirms that depression and anxiety are natural rites of passage – rites that get interrupted by chemical intervention.

And there is a clear reason for this: antidepressants and anxiolytics disrupt the brain's ability to learn about itself. Research at the Stanford University School of Medicine has shown that medication does not prevent a high activation of the HPA-axis (i.e. hyperarousal), but actually just makes one oblivious to it. During a test, chemically "tranquilized" anxious fliers, who reported feeling fine during a flight, had higher heart and breathing rates than un-tranquilized anxious fliers on the same flight who were in a state of panic! So, even though you may be unaware of the hyperarousal, it is nonetheless believed to traumatize the nervous system and increase its sensitization.[3]

And that is why these pills are so more-ish! Yet, despite the danger of addiction and the various other risks associated with anti-anxiety medication, I can also attest from personal experience that they do bring instant relief – much-needed when you have been hammered by your own adrenalin for days on end and just need a break. But they sure do not make you feel good – like most psychotropic medication, they tend to bestow a dull, depthless feeling of "flatland." What's worse, is that running to medication at the merest flutter of fear, reinforces (almost validates) the fight-or-flight response. With these drugs, in a subtle way, we are encouraged to fight our own fight-or-flight response, which is

---

[2] *Anatomy of an Epidemic* and *Mad in America* by Pulitzer Prize nominee Robert Whitaker
[3] www.ncbi.nlm.nih.gov/pubmed/9299803

like trying to douse a fire with petrol. We do not learn how to relax, or how to de-escalate the arousal, but rather expect a pill to do it for us.

And yet, as we have seen, the pill merely fools you into false security, making you oblivious to the anxiety raging away under the surface. It is the epitome of symptom relief that leaves you further from the cure.

The notion upon which the popularity of these drugs precariously teeters is that of "chemical imbalance." To be frank, this phrase is a marketing ploy, not a scientific statement. It arose from the backward reasoning that, because antidepressants increase the neurochemical serotonin, the problem must have been low serotonin. However, the low serotonin hypothesis has not held up to investigation, despite still being widely advertized. Studies were done to see whether or not depressed people actually had lower serotonin levels, and back in 1983 the National Institute of Mental Health in the US concluded: "There is no evidence that there is anything wrong in the serotonergic system of depressed patients."

It has also been demonstrated that, to the fractional degree that selective serotonin reuptake *inhibitors* (SSRIs, or antidepressants) can be said to work better than placebo, so can selective serotonin reuptake *enhancers*.[4] Suffice it to say, something is amiss.

No, unfortunately there is no magic bullet to cure anxiety or solve stress. But the good news is we do not need one, because there is no rush. A long-term stressful lifestyle is definitely your greatest health hazard, but thankfully stress is a really slow killer. Generally, the problem can be described as "chronic" rather than "acute" – and while the allopathic approach can be stunningly effective for acute crises, chronic conditions seem to fare better with a more holistic approach. And that is precisely why I prefer natural methods for resolving chronic anxiety.

Consider: Method X works for one out of ten people with a problem. Method X is cheap (or free) and has absolutely no side effects and is good for your body, even if it does not resolve the problem for nine out of ten people. On the other hand, Method Y works for nine out of ten people. It can be costly, has unpredictable side effects, and is not healthy, even when no obvious side effects seem to manifest. I would say try Method X first, and keep Method Y as a last resort. And that is why I maintain that "anecdotal evidence" has tremendous value.

I cannot thank an antidepressant for saving my life, but I am grateful to the angel that forced me to face my worst fears and come to terms

---

[4] *The Emperor's New Drugs* by Irving Kirsch. Basic Books, 2011

with them, to confront the madness of my mind, and to lose some delusions along the way. Jung wrote:

> "The reader will doubtless ask: What in the world is the value and meaning of a neurosis, this most useless and pestilent curse of humanity? To be neurotic – what good can that do? ... I myself have known more than one person who owed his whole usefulness and reason for existence to a neurosis, which prevented all the worst follies in his life and forced him to a mode of living that developed his valuable potentialities. These might have been stifled had not the neurosis, with iron grip, held him to the place where he belonged."

Disclaimer

Many people who seek my help with their anxiety are on medication, and I have seen remarkable transformation in even the most severe cases and the most heavily medicated – after they have come off the medication. If you are taking medication, the process of growth is still right there, waiting for you (with the Angel of Fear no doubt in attendance). It is simply a slower walk down a longer path. But please, if you decide that you want to come off your medication, *never* just quit outright. Be patient, and do it slowly over a long period, at increments. Find someone who inspires confidence and can give you ongoing support. And then, don't expect the process to be smooth – it is almost never smooth, even for those who are not coming off medication. Above all, do not stop your medication based on an author's opinion, or because you think you should. Only do it if you genuinely want to, on your own account, for your own reasons.

LET'S DO IT ♦ Better Pills

Not all pills are bitter. Magnesium has already been recommended in Chapter 1. But several other supplements are shown to be remarkably effective at improving your wellbeing and helping the body recover naturally from anxiety, or creating resilience to fight stress. Just don't get neurotic about it! Acceptance is the cure, but the following is a list of effective aids to help you. Give some of these options a try when you can afford it. Even if you do not feel fast symptom relief, it will not be money wasted. Your body will benefit – they are good for you.

Omega-3

Ongoing studies continue to suggest that omega-3s may be among the most effective antidepressant substances ever discovered. I won't bore you with the details – simply type *omega-3* and *anxiety* into an online search engine. Several of these studies hail from Harvard where clinicians have started using omega-3 supplements, and the results are encouraging.

Chronic inflammation is now correlated with depression and anxiety. While prolonged stress increases this inflammation, there is no doubt that countering the inflammation itself proves helpful. A high ratio of plant-based omega-6 oils compared to omega-3 has been shown to create systemic inflammation in the body. Scientists believe our ancestors had the perfect ratio of 1-to-1 omega-3 and omega-6, but now the balance is between 1-to-10 and 1-to-20 under the typical Western diet. This mismatch may explain why depression rates are so much lower in Asian countries where fish and seafood consumption is the highest. In fact, across the globe, countries with high levels of omega-3 consumption are correlated with low rates of depression.

It is estimated that the consumption of omega-3 in the West is *less than half* of what it was before WWII... and it is precisely since that period that rates of anxiety and depression have risen considerably. Our brains consist of 60% DHA, which is an animal-based omega-3 fat, and the brain needs a steady supply of omega-3s to function properly.

Harvard psychiatrist Andrew Stoll was one of the early leaders in compiling the evidence in support of animal-based omega-3 fats for the alleviation of depression and anxiety. His book *The Omega-3 Connection* details his experience.

People hear this and start eating more fish indiscriminately. Unfortunately, many types of fatty fish around the world now have dangerous levels of mercury, but sardines and pilchards are low enough on the aquatic food chain to be a good, clean and sustainable source of omega-3. (I make a delicious pilchard and sweet potato curry: Boil, peel and mash a few sweet potatoes. Add a can of pilchards with the sauce rinsed off. Then add lots of Tabasco sauce, and voila – easy, delicious and nutritious.)

Also worth noting is that the *New England Journal of Medicine* reports that free-range eggs contain 20 times more omega-3 than battery-farmed eggs.

Probiotics

Some scientists are calling our guts our "second brain," and the health of our intestinal bacteria, or microbiome, has a profound impact on our mental wellbeing.

We may already know this – we associate the gut with instinctive emotions and reactions. Gut reactions. When we are stressed, this is likely to be the first place we will feel the symptoms. In sympathetic nervous system activation, the body shuts down its energy-sapping digestive processes to divert energy for fight or flight. Persistent stress therefore means our gut never gets the chance to do its job properly. Stress alters the structure of our microbiome, while gut bacteria can in turn affect our stress responses.

There is a link between mental or emotional distress and a lack of natural micro-organisms in the gut. Many neurologists believe an imbalanced microbiome could be contributing to everything from Alzheimer's to autism. Their patients see dramatic improvements with an altered diet. They cut carbohydrates and add healthy fats, especially cholesterol – a key player in brain and psychological health. 'I've watched this fundamental dietary shift single-handedly extinguish depression and all of its kissing cousins, from chronic anxiety to poor memory and even ADHD," says one.

It seems our lives are over-sanitized, and we lack exposure to bacteria, both outside and inside our bodies. Pasteurization is another contentious issue that has robbed us of our natural symbiotic relationship with micro-organisms. Fermented foods used to be traditional staples in most cultures, but modern food manufacturing with its fearful focus on food safety has contributed to the reduction in use of most of these foods. In most health shops you should still be able to find traditionally fermented foods like kefir or natto, but they simply are not the dietary staples they once were. Depriving ourselves of all bacteria means our immune systems – our primary defence against inflammation – gets weaker, not stronger.

While you can strive to include fermented vegetables (like sauerkraut, or unpasteurized miso) in your diet to promote healthy intestinal flora, it is probably a grand idea to take a probiotic supplement from time to time. There is actually more serotonin in your gut than in your brain, and a probiotic supplement will help normalize the production of neurotransmitters that are responsible for optimal brain functioning.

B's and C's
A good vitamin B complex is also known to be a good stress-buster, while vitamin C supports the kidneys and adrenals, as they can get exhausted from all that adrenalin production!

5HTP
This is an effective serotonin precursor. While I doubt the "low serotonin" theory of depression, adrenalin and serotonin are actually antagonists in your body. The more adrenalin, the less serotonin, and vice versa. I recommend the most natural type, which is griffonia seed extract – provided you are not already on an antidepressant.

Herbs
Sceletium is a natural South African mood elevator that has been used for centuries, originally by the Khoisan. Choose a variety that has all the whole compounds, not just extracts. You can also try sceletium tea. Other calming herbs include passiflora, chamomile (highly underrated) and valerian (which apparently can make some people a bit *more* anxious). Experiment and see what resonates with your system over time. Some people also swear by Rescue Remedy.

Reduce inflammation
As mentioned, depression and anxiety have been strongly linked to systemic, low-grade inflammation in the body. There are two powerful natural solutions to this – *zinc* is one of nature's most powerful anti-inflammatories, and so is *turmeric*. With the current state of global soil depletion, we are not likely to be getting the same amounts of magnesium and zinc as our grandparents got from food. Use lots of turmeric in scrambled eggs in the morning, as well as in soups and curries and stir fries. However, we do not absorb much of it unless we add a pinch of black pepper! Whenever you use turmeric, add pepper – you do not need much; even a pinch makes most of the turmeric you eat highly absorbable.

7

WHEN PANIC ATTACKS

In the predawn desert of New Mexico, 1945, observers were plunged into collective darkness as they donned their goggles in the moments before detonation. With the countdown approaching zero, some remembered that they had bet good money that their bunkers would be obliterated. Others had wagered that the blast would ignite the atmosphere and incinerate the entire planet.

That first flash would herald a new age. At the nearest camp 16km away, the surrounding mountains were lit up "brighter than daytime," and the heat was "as hot as an oven." A giant cloud mushroomed 12km into the sky, while windows were rattled and the sound of the explosion could be heard more than 300km away.

After some euphoria at their success (and survival, no doubt), test director Kenneth Bainbridge turned to his colleague J. Robert Oppenheimer and noted: "Now we are all sons of bitches." Oppenheimer, of a more poetic bent and fluent in Sanskrit, recalled a line from the *Bhagavad-Gita*: *Now I am become Death, the destroyer of worlds.*

The Trinity test, as this first atomic explosion was called, signalled one of the most significant developments in human history. It brought our last world war to a swift end, and kept future world wars cold, thanks to assured mutual destruction. The bomb and the nuclear energy that followed was a pinnacle of scientific achievement, and the dawn of the Atomic Age was a triumph of the rational mind.

That explosion would come to echo through our culture, and along with the Atomic Age rose the Age of Anxiety, announced in no uncertain terms in W.H. Auden's Pulitzer Prize-winning poem by the same name in 1947. The poem deals with the quest to find depth and meaning in an increasingly industrialized, flatland world, and the female protagonist conjures with prescience our current time:

> "Odourless ages, an ordered world
> Of planned pleasures and passport-control,
> Sentry-go sedatives, soft drinks and
> Managed money, a moral planet
> Tamed by terror…"

TRICKSY HOBBITS

"The news today about 'Atomic Bombs' is so horrifying one is stunned," wrote J.R.R. Tolkien in a letter shortly after the Trinity test. "The utter folly of these lunatic physicists to consent to do such work for war-purposes: calmly plotting the destruction of the world!"[5] His sentiments were shared by many pre-eminent intellectuals at the time.

Tolkien was a mild eccentric with an intense dislike of industrialization, which he felt was devouring the English countryside and the simple life. Disdainful of cars, he preferred to ride a bicycle. He believed mythology to be the divine echoes of eternal truths, and that fairy stories allowed readers to review their own world from a fresh perspective – he saw its potential for uncovering and changing unquestioned cultural assumptions.

In a letter to his friend W.H. Auden, Tolkien recalls how the story of *The Hobbit* came to him. He was marking school papers when he came across a blank page and, suddenly inspired, wrote the words: "In a hole in the ground there lived a hobbit." It is one of the great opening lines in literature. The simplicity is pure haiku.

Tolkien created a world of talking trees and elves, and in so doing sought to defend the imagination and "the wonder of things, such as stone, and wood, and iron; tree and grass; house and fire; bread and wine." He feared the dangers of modern technology and often called it "orc-ery," and although he disliked allegory for its literal-mindedness, he

---

[5] A letter to his son Christopher Tolkien, 9 August 1945, who, in response to the much later film versions of his father's books, would lament: "Tolkien has become a monster, devoured by his own popularity and absorbed into the absurdity of our time. The chasm between the beauty and seriousness of the work, and what it has become, has overwhelmed me. The commercialization has reduced the aesthetic and philosophical impact of the creation to nothing. There is only one solution for me: to turn my head away." (*Le Monde*)

did concede that the titular ring in *The Lord of the Rings* was akin to the corrupting power of the Machine, in whatever form. In the trilogy, the evil Sauron seeks to industrialize the world and conquer nature. And the closer the hobbits get to Sauron's land of Mordor, the greater their anxiety and dread.

As Auden's former professor, Tolkien's principle concerns are an apt clue to our Age of Anxiety. "I saw ages long past," said Tolkien in a speech, "when still trees bloomed free in a wide country. Alas, for now all begins to wither in the breath of cold-hearted wizards. To know things, they break them. And their stern lordship they establish through the fear of death."

For Tolkien, the tragedy of the age was the "scouring of the Shire" – the ruin of unexploited nature in its pure form. The Shire is the land of hobbits, who, above all, live in harmony with the natural world. The country-loving hobbits have hairy feet, live in cave-like "holes" and go about mostly unseen by humans. In many ways, they are much like another icon of rustic nature…

THE GREAT GOD PAN

Tolkien's hobbits share a similar spirit to the Greek god of nature, Pan. Half man, half goat, Pan sleeps in caves and dwells only in the wild, rarely to be seen. On his birth in the pristine land of Arcadia, it is said that his mother was so frightened by the beard and goat horns that she abandoned him. His father, Hermes, wrapped him in a pelt and took him to Mount Olympus, where the gods welcomed him warmly.

As a figure symbolic of "nature alive," a renewal of popular and academic interest in Pan coincided with the rise of the Atomic Age, and the goat-god became an icon for those who lamented "the Fall into civilization."[6]

Our word *panic* comes from the Greek *panikos*, derived from the name of the god Pan. Following the Industrial Revolution, the emergence of an undefined type of fright prompted the coining of a new medical condition, for which the popular term today is *panic attack*. This phenomenon was first called "Panophobia."

When Jung famously said that "the gods have become diseases," he was pointing out that the gods of mythology represent our psychic

---

[6] In his book on postmodernism, *After the Orgy*, Dominic Pettman writes: "In the 1960s, when the sexual revolution cannot be distinguished from the fear of nuclear Armageddon…, the iconic resurgence of Pan signalled uneasy anxiousness as well as hedonistic promiscuity."

energies. "We are still as much possessed today by autonomous psychic contents as if they were Olympians. Today they are called phobias, obsessions, and so forth; in a word, neurotic symptoms."

Understanding Pan's relevance in the human psyche can give us insight, not only into panic, but into the values that are trying to come into consciousness. "For where panic is, there too is Pan," writes the great depth psychologist James Hillman, who recommends that we not suppress the energy of the trickster, but learn of his nature.

Pan played a significant role in pagan Greek and Roman worship, in various guises, and the ancient peoples who recognized Pan as alive were deeply connected to the ways of nature, in both their inner and outer realities. Hillman says that Pan "is still alive, although we experience him only through psychopathological disturbances, other modes having been lost in our culture." When we ignore Pan, his power erupts to catch our attention.

Hillman insists that aspects of Pan's nature are therapeutic to the soul.[7] He even defends panic as a valid, valuable experience, and says: "Fear, like love, can become a call into consciousness." To propitiate Pan is to answer that call. For starters then, let us seek a reconciliation with kin, as did the biblical Jacob, and consider that panic, like evolution, is *natural*.

BACK TO NATURE

With atomic clouds sprouting all over the place after the Trinity test, man had picked a dangerous mushroom. And Pan said: not so fast. Through our rocketing rates of anxiety and panic since the mid-20th century, Pan has been calling us back to nature – back to our instincts, and our dreams where instinct has free reign.

Tolkien's fantasy was a response, not to technology and science per se, but to the dangers of such developments without commensurate interior evolution – ethical, psychological, spiritual, imaginal. Without balance, Pan brings the backlash, and our one-sided worship of Reason will tend to make us sick.

---

[7] Hillman elaborates: "The importance of technology and scientific knowledge for protecting nature's processes goes without saying, but part of the ecological field is human nature, in whose psyche the archetypes dominate. If Pan is suppressed there, nature and instinct will go astray no matter how we strain on rational levels to set things right. In order to restore, conserve and promote nature 'out there', nature 'in here' must also be restored, conserved and protected to precisely the same degree." (*Pan and the Nightmare*)

Illustrations of this abound – sanitization has saved us from contagions, but its excess is implicated in epidemics of mental distress (see previous chapter); hospitals undeniably save lives, but the medical system is ironically one of our leading causes of death and injury,[8] in some estimations even outstripping the other top causes, like heart disease and cancer; computers have brought convenience, but sitting in front of a screen for hours daily is now considered as unhealthy as smoking… Added examples could fill a book.

No wonder people turn to "alternative medicine" – a move toward nature. Arguably, Tolkien's "cold-hearted wizards" wore white coats and treated all beings as biological machines. These reductionists employ the mystic-sounding *imbalance* to explain our panic, but insist that this imbalance is random, and chemical. And so they counsel us to swallow more of precisely what is making us sick in the first place.

The real imbalance at the core of our problems with panic is too much Apollo, not enough Pan. It is the monotheistic worship of Reason and dismissal of the trans-rational revelations of the nature mystics. It is the way economists bracket the natural world off outside its equations as "externalities." It is our conspicuous consumption, our factory farming, our foot always on the accelerator, speeding away from Arcadia.

This imbalance has resulted in a back-to-nature backlash. A radical response has come from the "deep ecologists," Neo-Luddites and anarcho-primitivists, but more moderately, ever-growing numbers of city slickers imagine escaping urban sprawl for some version of an eco-village. And it only seems natural – in 1800, only 3% of the world's population lived in cities. Today it is well over 50%.

The Findhorn Foundation in Scotland has spearheaded the eco-village movement since the mid-1990s, with its own eco-village boasting a Best Practice award from the UN Centre for Human Settlements (HABITAT). Findhorn has become a globally recognized symbol of living in harmony with nature, thanks in large part to the books of co-founder Robert Crombie, who had abandoned his career as a scientist due to ill health and retreated from city life to the countryside. Unusually attuned to nature, Crombie wrote at length about having personal, visionary encounters with Pan.

On a personal level, though, we do not need to up sticks and join a commune to honour Pan. We can simply reconnect with nature. And while this reconnection does not need to be literal, taking ourselves into actual nature might be a good place to start. In fact, aside from the fresh

---

[8] www.webdc.com/pdfs/deathbymedicine.pdf

air, exercise and visual beauty, nature restores mental functioning through what psychologists call *attention restoration theory* (ART).

According to ART, there is a fundamental difference between urban and natural landscapes in the way they affect our minds. The way urban environments grab our attention (from traffic to advertising) is generally draining to the nervous system – a constant barrage of *look here, now look there, read this, buy that, mind the gap*! Natural environments, on the other hand, have a replenishing effect on our mental resources in the way they induce a soft, diffuse type of attention, much like the open awareness that mindfulness meditation aims to cultivate. This is but one mechanism through which nature provides significant benefits, from medical outcomes to workplace productivity.

In both Japan and Germany, the tradition of natural therapy is well established. The Japanese version is known as *shinrin-yoku*, or "forest bathing," which places patients in forested areas for extended periods. German Kneipp therapy similarly sees patients perform physical exercises in forest clearings. It is worth recognizing that these therapies are not merely alternative quirks based on cultural tradition. The very building blocks of our wellbeing respond positively to natural therapy, from lowering blood pressure to lowering pulse rates to lowering cortisol levels – all markers of reduced stress and anxiety.

Earthing

Cape Town offered a measure of easy access to nature that really helped in my recovery from anxiety. The city and its suburbs are nestled at the foot of the Table Mountain chain. With endless hiking trails, a new natural scene unfolds around every corner – pine forest, indigenous jungle, fynbos. The mountain itself is older than the Himalayas, and more biodiverse than the Amazon basin. Ancient Khoisan tribes called it *Hoerikwaggo* – Sea Mountain – because it is surrounded by ocean. Tidal pools punctuate some of the world's most beautiful beaches and dramatic coastline. I was lucky to have Pan's domain at hand.

In the move from the man-made world to nature, our relationship to the outer environment changes from one of consumption to communion – we are not just passive observers, but are called to engage. An exchange takes place that is not based on trade.

One example of this exchange may be electric. Proponents of earthing, or grounding, claim that when we walk barefoot on a beach or swim in the sea, we benefit from the Earth's reservoir of negatively charged free electrons. Some intriguing research has suggested that connecting to the earth, skin to skin as it were, confers immense benefits to both physical and mental health.

It allows the cells in our brains and bodies to balance the positive charge that results from electron-deficient free radicals. Because of rubber soles on shoes, and the insulation of indoor flooring and our sleeping arrangements, most of us fail to benefit from the powerful anti-inflammatory effect of being "grounded." This inflammation may be exacerbated by constant bombardment with electromagnetic radiation from computers, mobile phones and masts. WiFi, Bluetooth, power lines, domestic wiring, and other electrical appliances cause voltages in our bodies that disrupt the trillions of subtle electrical communications between our cells. One of the effects of grounding can be seen clearly under a microscope in the beneficial way blood cells behave.

Much of the advantage I got from going to the beach, swimming in the ocean, and walking barefoot in the mountains may have come from this positive charge grounding out, while I absorbed the Earth's beneficial negative ions. Earthing has also been shown to dramatically improve heart-rate variability, lower cortisol, improve blood viscosity, and sleep – strongly reducing the biological markers of stress. It reportedly has several beneficial effects on the brain.

That said, it must be noted that the research in this field is still in its infancy, and like most areas of health, there is some contention, with sceptics being sceptical, and believers underestimating the placebo effect. While I would not yet recommend buying earthing bed-sheets or grounding yourself through an electrical socket, the research that has been done so far certainly seems promising, and suggests the need for further stringent investigation.

As the earthing movement continues to grow, with many people reporting great benefit, I cannot help but wonder if the psychological significance of earthing outweighs the issues around its scientific validity. It seems an expression of a collective desire to reconnect to the Earth. Walking barefoot brings us to our senses, and our attention down from our heads. It *feels* good. There is a ritual element to going outside and taking off one's shoes – a ritual that makes for a happy Pan.

THE INNER OUTDOORS

When we explore Pan's domain, we would do best to keep practising an attitude of acceptance. Pan is clever and can sniff out plots to get rid of panic. Remember that panic is rooted in human nature, and therefore is no aberration. "That fear, dread, and horror are natural is wisdom," says Hillman. Wanting to get rid of panic, although also quite natural, is no way to honour Pan. But, over time, panic can be replaced with some of Pan's other passions.

Whenever we allow the crazy chaos of the creative right brain to temper the calculating left brain, with its one-sided take on truth, Pan is pleased. Our return to nature does not only need to be literal. We can connect with Pan internally, and panic itself hints at the way.

The god was discerned in nature when a herd would suddenly get spooked and bolt. Herds do not have to wait for proof of danger – a suspicious rustle is enough to trigger flight. Panic is just that – before we know what set us off, our hearts are hoofing it. This is Pan as the trickster.

Panic is usually fed by storylines that linger in the subliminal mind. We feel that panic strikes "out of nowhere," but when we learn to recognize the activity of the subliminal mind (through mindfulness practice, for example), we can begin to see these whispered storylines and how they set us up. These narratives, or subtle superstitions, whisper "what ifs," and resistance kicks in. The subliminal mind is much stronger than the surface mind with its discursive thoughts, and so when it suggests we may be at risk of losing control, the mind spins into panic in a matter of seconds. Because loss of control must be resisted at all costs. And so, panic is yet another of fear's self-fulfilling loops – a panic attack is fear of a panic attack. I almost never have panic attacks anymore, because I really do not mind if I do. But of course it took me a long time to learn not to mind.

The storyline in the subliminal mind that kicks it all off is usually one of two variations on the theme of absolute loss of control.

First is the fundamental fear of death. We sense imminent annihilation in multicolour melodrama, in visions of accidents, heart attacks, suicides. Death can seem like the final reduction – dust to dust. But the Grim Reaper is in Pan's employ, as nature's ultimate non-negotiable. After all, it is only natural – no one here gets out alive.

It might honour Pan if we were to study grief and dying, volunteer at a hospice, or read about near-death research. But when fantasies of abrupt death hound us, the message is not meant to be taken literally. In order to move up the spiral of psychological development, to be reborn into a wider view, an expanded consciousness, we must die to our sense of self and let go of all orientations and certainties. This will give the feeling of literally being in mortal danger. We are indeed dying, but not physically. Instead, it is the contraction before the expansion – a natural rhythm that has been called "regression in the service of transcendence."[9]

The second storyline or superstition is the fear of going insane. As if a momentary dizziness might tip us into a full-blown derangement. Fine one moment, bonkers the next. Before you know it, you are being tackled on the front lawn by orderlies as the neighbours look on. Then off to the loony bin, with Thorazine for supper.

This fear is surprisingly common. Losing one's faculties spells an ultimate loss of control, and its resultant shame. That is not a pleasant prospect when we're always trying to be on top of everything. Guilt often plays an important role here – we may harbour an unseen belief that God is out to get us. We have been bad, or have failed in some fundamental way, and we are to be punished. It has just been biding its time.

This is our imagination playing tricks. Boil it right down and this fear of madness is a dread of the chaotic forces of the unconscious. Yes, Pan is at play here. To the strictly rational, "civilized" mind, he is a force of the creative world of dreams and nightmares.

When we frighten ourselves with these kind of thoughts, we might connect with Pan by learning about the non-rational mind. In *The Meaning of Anxiety*, an intellectual history of anxiety by the famous existential psychologist Rollo May, the author asks the question: "Why did anxiety not emerge as a specific problem until the middle of the 19th century?" Published in 1950, *The Meaning of Anxiety* was a landmark book, preceded only by two previous studies into anxiety – an essay by Freud and one by Kierkegaard. To answer the question, Rollo May says: "One of the many legitimate answers is our widespread tendency ... to look askance at 'irrational' phenomena. We tend to admit only those aspects of experience that can be made to appear 'rational'."

During darker days, it was my deep-seated fear of the irrational mind – imagined as madness – that hounded me most. I merely had to read the word *psychosis* for an atomic bomb to go off in my brain. And the more I avoided the subject, the more it generated a dreaded mix of fear and fascination. When I finally understood that the way to recovery would be to face my fears, and come to terms with them, I realized it meant I would have to study the nature of madness. In doing so, it led to disabusing myself of some naïve notions about so-called insanity. I saw that the various versions of "crazy" are simply amplifications of our

---

[9] In his book *The Ego and the Dynamic Ground*, transpersonal psychologist Michael Washburn refers to heightened neuroses as "regression in the service of transcendence." This phrase captures Pan's dual nature, from goat (regression) to god (transcendence).

workaday delusions and mental habits. I learnt that I was already quite mad, and had simply been in denial!

This fear of madness is so widespread that I asked my friend and respected author Rob Nairn to add his insights to this book. As one of the principal pioneers in bringing mindfulness and Buddhist dharma to southern Africa, Rob's signature clarity is perfectly suited to the topic. See Appendix A for his contribution on the subject.

CATCHING Z'S

So, we can honour the god Pan by becoming more familiar with the non-rational mind. I have found that the best way to do this is to pay attention to night-time dreams by keeping a dream journal. Resisting the impulse to *interpret* dreams also loosens our grip on literal-mindedness, as we engage the dream on its own terms. Paying attention to the unconscious, its threat diminishes. On the contrary, the imagination extends its domain, our sub-personalities begin to feel seen, and consciousness expands as self-acceptance begins to circulate.

Pan is a dreamer. He loves his sleep, and so we also tend to do well when we harmonize our internal clocks to the most basic rhythm of nature – day and night. You can have a sterling diet and exercise programme, but without proper sleep you can still become depressed and anxious. Sleep and depression are so intimately linked that sleep problems are considered symptomatic of clinical depression.

One of many recent studies highlighted the crucial role of adequate rest in managing stress by measuring the effects of sleep deprivation on a number of healthy young participants who were allowed to sleep for only four hours per night, six nights in a row. They exhibited significantly increased cortisol levels, including at times when they were supposedly relaxing and taking a break.[10]

Lack of sleep causes both physical and mental stress, causing inflammation, and making it that much harder to get adequate sleep the next night, since you know that stress will directly alter your ability to sleep – a typical vicious cycle. When you do not get enough sleep for one night your immune system will be activated, leading to the production of inflammatory markers like interleukin-6, which targets the central nervous system and can even trigger fever – that is how powerful its effect is. The inflammatory markers in turn raise cortisol and other

---

[10] *Revue Neurologique*, 2006

stress hormone levels, producing more stress and damaging cells and telomeres (which are attached to the end of each chromosome and protect both the chromosome and the cell from becoming cancerous). Lack of sleep will cause stress in a surprisingly short period of time, and the effects on your mental and physical performance will be significant.

Sleep researchers say that when we routinely fail to get enough sleep, we accumulate what is called a "sleep debt" – a compromising deficit that many of us carry around unawares. Thomas Wehr is one such researcher, famous for identifying Seasonal Affective Disorder (SAD) in the 1990s, and developing light therapy to treat it. He was researching the effects of light and sleep on seasonal depression when he wondered what would happen if humans were forced to follow the rhythms of nature, with no recourse to artificial light.

For the first few nights, all the subjects slept much more than normal, averaging about 11 hours a night. One interesting finding about sleep debt is that you cannot clear it in one lump sum. It takes nightly instalments over a period of about two to three weeks to pay off. Once this debt had been settled, however, Wehr's volunteers all stabilized into a pattern of about eight hours a night, on average.

Our sleep cycle is bio-chemically programmed to kick in an hour or two after it gets dark, and forcing wakefulness beyond this point puts stress on the whole system. The problem is that you cannot undo the distress on your system by sleeping late the next morning. While you may ultimately still get your eight hours of sleep, the body's internal clock will be distressed. When you ignore the natural sleep cycle, the body produces stress hormones to keep you awake. So when you regularly have late nights, your body adapts to the anticipated stress by secreting stress-coping hormones automatically every night. You cannot play catch-up with just a few nights of going to bed early. The body has to be coached back to its natural rhythm over a period of weeks.

When the internal clock is out of whack, sunshine helps to get it back on track. The brain has a light gauge, and unless it gets sunshine for at least a solid hour of exposure every day, it throws off the circadian rhythms, which regulate sleep, energy and hormones. Besides which, sunlight is the best source of vitamin D, far better than supplements, and those with a deficiency in this crucial vitamin tend to score much higher on anxiety and depression tests than those with healthy levels. Sunlight's beneficial effects on mood are well documented. (Keep in mind: the UVA/UVB ratio of sunlight is negatively altered by glass, so try not to tan through a closed window.)

Adequate sunlight or not, we still tend to burn the candle at both ends, thanks to that character Thomas Edison, who always boasted that he never slept more than three hours a night (although he made up for it with many impromptu naps during the day). Exposure to artificial light exerts a profound suppressive effect on the sleep hormone melatonin, causing a cascade of negative outcomes that range from blood pressure to glucose homeostasis.

Worse than normal artificial light is the light emitted from devices like laptops and iPads. One recent study showed that, when participants used an iPad at night, their pineal glands produced 55% less melatonin compared to reading a book on paper, and they got less REM sleep during the night. The next morning, they felt sleepier, and it took "hours longer" for them to feel alert. But here's the kicker – at bedtime the next night, the iPad readers' internal clocks were delayed by a full 90 minutes, due to their exposure from the night before.[11]

Often we are not getting enough bright daylight exposure during the day, while at night we are getting too much artificial light exposure. And then we become so accustomed to the resulting attention deficit and subpar cognition, we mistake it for normal. No wonder Pan is angry – he's groggy from not enough sleep!

For an easy summary on how to counteract this dire state of affairs, see the sleep recommendations at the end of this chapter.

WWPD – WHAT WOULD PAN DO?

We have explored a few of the factors from Pan's domain that we often neglect. But the number of ways we can please Pan and return to nature, figuratively speaking, is limited only by our imaginations. Even something as simple as a change in diet, from processed foods, to whole or raw foods, is a big step in the right direction. You cannot go wrong with a daily kale salad with goat's-milk feta!

Learning about the Taoist way of concord with nature is another powerful and practical path toward Pan. Besides a fondness for panpipes, the Greek god and the Chinese tradition share the premise that health and harmony result when human nature is aligned with the rest of nature. Whether it is through Tai Chi, chi kung, or the sexual practices of Taoist tantra, it is an endlessly rich and rewarding path that will undoubtedly placate panic and help resolve anxiety.

On a different note, Pan is also found in many forms of art, from

---

[11] www.pnas.org/content/112/4/1232.full.pdf

the contemporary nature poetry of Mary Oliver to the Romantic movement of the 19th century. Romanticism developed as an intellectual and artistic antithesis to the effects of the Industrial Revolution. Its major exponents included William Blake and the poets Wordsworth, Coleridge, Keats, Lord Byron and Shelley. Shelley's wife Mary wrote *Frankenstein*, which reflected the concern that scientific progress is double-edged. In fine art, music and literature, the movement stressed the value of wild nature, in contrast to early urban sprawl and the growth of factories – Blake's "dark satanic mills."

The movement accentuated intense emotion, and placed special emphasis on the darker feelings like apprehension, fear and awe – especially in relation to the beauty of nature, and the special mix of danger and wonder that describes the sublime. Romantics distrusted the man-made world, and tended to assert that a close connection with nature was mentally and morally healthy.

The Romantic movement gave birth to another artistic movement by the late 19th century. Symbolism arose as a reaction to the rationalism and materialism of the time, and also emphasized the validity of emotions. It favoured subjectivity – spirituality, imagination, dreams – while marrying mysticism with the perverse and erotic. A perfect combination of Pan-ic qualities.

Arguably the leader of the new Symbolist movement was the painter Paul Gauguin, who lamented the spiritual decline of the modern world and gave up his lucrative career as a stockbroker to paint full time and eventually move to Tahiti. He was known for lecturing his fellow artists on the importance of returning to nature and painting as if in a dream. "Give me the country," he wrote. "I love Brittany; I find in it the savage and the primitive."

Gauguin's renown among artistic contemporaries came with his work *Vision After the Sermon* (a detail of which serves as the cover for this book). It exemplified his interest in a new aesthetic as a result of his travels to Brittany and Martinique, where he sought to live in harmony with nature. Few paintings of the period have inspired more analysis and speculation, and it has been praised as the greatest of Gauguin's works, unlocking what would become almost all of 20th-century art. In his own lifetime, the painting was described as giving the initiated access to hidden mysteries.

So Pan, I'd say, loves a pretty painting. And, despite being demonized, I would hazard a guess that he is rather fond of angels too (see Chapter 11).

LET'S DO IT ♦ Tech Cold Turkey

Tolkien had misgivings about our notions of progress, which we invariably measure in the advance from tools to tech. But his contemporary, the economist John Maynard Keynes, was more optimistic, predicting that technical progress would soon solve mankind's economic problems, and that "man will be faced with his real, permanent problem – how to use his freedom from pressing economic cares, how to occupy the leisure, which science and compound interest will have won for him…" If only.

But we cannot blame Tolkien's "wizards." We are quite complicit, and cannot seem to help ourselves. Always advertised to save us time, we allow our tech to up the pace, and addict ourselves to digital distractions, prioritizing productivity to such a degree that we become *hyperemployed* (a term coined by contemporary media theorist Ian Bogost). Most often, however, we simply mistake busy for productive. If we had "more time" in our lives – let's face it – we might easily fill it with Facebook.

We think of ourselves as "connected," when in fact we are increasingly disconnected from nature, and from each other. Modern life is filled with distraction, and our attention deficit is close to tipping point. Every new post, listicle, snippet or selfie stimulates the reward centres in our brain, and is creating a hungry network of neurological receptors. The scroll bar is like a dopamine drip. Conditioned to constant novelty and a non-stop diet of low-calorie info, we are literally becoming addicted to our own biochemistry.

Tech-addiction has become a recognized problem, and I have met many people who really struggle with downtime. When you become anxious when you do not receive a constant stream of stimuli, it forces you to mindlessly seek it from various devices – the TV or laptop being reliable sources.

Our brains can become so accustomed to incoming information that we release stress chemicals when something new fails to materialize. TV and other devices deliver new stimuli constantly and reinforce the need for more, more, more. To short-circuit this cycle, try the following challenges to train your brain not to release the neurotransmitters that trigger stress and anxiety when things get quiet.

1. Set a random alarm, and when it goes off, switch off your phone, TV or laptop for at least 15 minutes. When you can do this without any discomfort, try 20, then 30. Sounds easy, but the catch is not to seek any

other entertainment. Notice the discomfort and "fear of missing out" and ask yourself if this feels natural and healthy.

2. Two or three times in the day, when something interesting but insignificant catches your attention online, choose *not* to click on it. The ten best photobombs of the year? Pass, and feel the burn.

3. For one whole week, whenever you visit Facebook, resist the urge to scroll. You can see your messages, upcoming events, and the first post to appear on your news feed, but that's it. No scrolling!

4. Reflect on your addiction to distraction, without any blame, shame or self-judgment. The point is obviously not to conclude that social media or technology is "bad," but simply to raise some questions. What are we sacrificing? Are we mistaking "connected" for connection?

LET'S DO IT ♦ Settle Your Sleep Debt

1. Spend at least an hour outdoors each day, preferably at midday. So-called "anchor light" anchors your biological rhythm, and it is the first hour that creates about 80% of the anchoring effect. So if you work in an office or indoors, try taking your lunch break outside.

2. Dim your house lights after sunset. Dimmer switches are a good investment.

3. Download the f.lux software for your computer, at Justgetflux.com, which will automatically reduce the melatonin-disrupting blue light wavelength on your laptop or iPad monitor after sunset. It's free.

4. Do not go to bed on a full stomach. Have your last meal about three hours before lights out.

5. Recharge during the day. The best way to do this? A 10-minute nap. So much research has been done on the benefits of napping, I think I'll give the footnotes a break and just sum up the general findings. First, 10 minutes seems to be the goldilocks zone. 20 or 30 minutes is good too, but its benefits do not last as long, and you may have to go through a short period of grogginess called "sleep inertia." Nap for more than 45 minutes, and you will likely disrupt your sleep cycle at night.

LET'S DO IT ♦ Dance Like No One Is Watching

The best antidote to the fear of madness, I have found, is to go mad – and this is best done by dancing!

As a god of the dance, Pan really loves a good boogie. Dancing is a natural human impulse with deep-rooted historical significance, from the ancient Greek worship of Dionysus to the medieval practice of Christianity as a "danced religion."

"Joy is in the feet," as the Lubavitcher Rebbe has said.

In the ancient past, dancing was often used to cure people of sadness, until literalist religions sought to suppress it – Protestants criminalized carnival, Wahhabist Muslims feared ecstatic Sufism, and European colonizers destroyed native dance rites. While it is natural to dance, it is a knack many of us have lost. With a Puritanical attitude having pervaded the world, many of us have difficulty loosening up in our bodies, needing alcohol just to be able to overcome the ego's defences against "looking silly." One could say we suffer from a lack of dancing in our lives.

Personally I find dancing complements the practice of meditation – it balances some of my Apollonian, ascetic tendencies with my often-neglected Dionisic, Pan-ic, wild nature. It unlocks energies and inner personalities that have been suppressed, and is undoubtedly therapeutic.

From 5Rhythms to Movement Medicine to BlissDance, there are a number of "conscious dance" groups that have gone global. I'm not sure ballet and ballroom will do – what's needed is something more formless. It's a good way to let the body seek its own pleasure through movement, without the head getting too much in the way. For further inspiration, Barbara Ehrenreich's *Dancing in the Streets: A History of Collective Joy* is a wonderful potted history of communal dance.

If dancing in a group doesn't float your boat, just do it at home alone. If not once a day for just one or two tracks, then perhaps once a week for a little more. Doctor's orders.

PART 3: FREEDOM FROM FEAR

8

LOVE'S LABOURS

A standstill bank queue often brings home to me a grim burden – the taming of testosterone. With my patience tested, I'll confess I have sometimes dreamt of pulling a Tommy gun from my trench coat to announce a robbery.

John Dillinger lived this dream. "All my life I wanted to be a bank robber," he said. "Now that it's happened I guess I'm just about the best bank robber they ever had. And I sure am happy."

With the Great Depression in full swing, happiness seemed a rare commodity in the early 1930s. and ordinary Americans fed vicariously off the thrill of Dillinger's exploits, making him a celebrity outlaw. Dillinger brought such flair to bank heists that newspapers were hard-pressed *not* to sensationalize. Banks in the Midwest were particularly gullible when he posed as a sales rep for an alarm system company, using the ruse to scope security measures and vaults. His popularity swelled when his gang posed as a film crew scouting locations for a bank robbery scene – a con which ended with bystanders ambling around smiling while Dillinger and his friends skipped off with the loot.

A pioneer in creative bank robbing, Dillinger was also arguably the product of desperate times and a flawed penal system. Newly married and struggling to find work in Indianapolis, the young Dillinger befriended a local pool shark, and together they robbed a grocer of $120. Thanks to a witness they were quickly apprehended. His friend pleaded not guilty and got sentenced to two years. Dillinger followed the advice of his conscientious father, also a grocer who had rarely spared the rod, and confessed. For his honesty Dillinger received joint sentences of fourteen and twenty years in the Indiana State Prison. Stunned by the harsh sentence, he pledged to become "the meanest bastard you ever saw" upon his eventual release.

Did a judge create Dillinger? As a youngster he was known for getting into scuffles and petty theft, but for a boy whose mother died just before his fourth birthday, and who was then left to the strictures of a harsh father and an antagonistic stepmother, such behaviour is no great mystery. When he was finally paroled eight and a half years later, with the best criminal education $120 could buy, he would seek to make good on his promise.

Within days he started on a crime spree of epic proportions. Witnesses were eager to report his words: "Now nobody get nervous, you ain't got nothing to fear. You're being robbed by the John Dillinger Gang, and that's the best there is!"

Today the FBI website refers to him as a "lurid desperado" and a "vicious thief" whose "violent gang terrorized the Midwest." But at the time, Dillinger stirred mass emotion and quickly became something of a folk hero, sticking it to the perceived baddies of the time – the bankers.

Ethics aside, I cannot help but admire how much Dillinger loved what he did. Robbing banks was not a means to an end – it was an end in itself. Although he stole enough cash to comfortably live out his days on a tropical beach, that was never the goal. Being a bank robber was his calling. And to live this, he had to learn to abide fear.

In our own lives, once we have recognized our calling (not necessarily synonymous with our career), we may feel great fear, but have to follow the call. There is a natural need for vitality and inspiration. Without these qualities, an anxious aridness can come to plague us, and our work life feels barren.

We need to find our inner John Dillinger. So that we can also say: "I sure am happy."

Money Money Money

As mentioned, the psychologist Rollo May asked why anxiety had not emerged as much of a recognizable phenomenon until the middle of the 19th century. While he failed to make a specific connection to the most obvious big change at the time – the Industrial Revolution – he did refer to industrialism in general:

> "One of the psychological results of industrialism is that

for the majority of people *work has lost its intrinsic meaning.* Work has become a 'job,' in which the criterion of value is not the productive or creative activity itself [...] but merely the acquisition of wealth. The value placed highest in the industrial system is the aggrandizement of wealth."[12]

The accumulation of obscene wealth has become one of the big issues of our time. Billionaires abound and the growing wealth gap is a hot topic. The irony is that the wealthy are essentially no happier than the rest. People who have it far better than most still feel imperilled and unsettled, because the very drive to accumulate wealth is so often fuelled by insecurity. A US banking poll in 2000 showed that 64% of super-rich Americans, with an average wealth of $38 million, feel "financially insecure"!

As we adhere to a philosophy of scarcity, while regarding the world as essentially hostile, it might seem that only money can allay our insecurities. There was a time when our ancestors performed ritual sacrifices to avert natural catastrophes. Today, the favoured rite for dodging disaster is to fatten the personal bank account. This appears to make the world only slightly safer than blood sacrifice, as nature always has the final say – from droughts to dread disease to freak accidents, we can never absolutely insulate ourselves.

Of course, being poor is stressful, while wealth per se is not bad; nor is striving to achieve it. It is a natural impulse – as the economist John Maynard Keynes noted:

> "The economic problem, the struggle for subsistence, always has been hitherto the primary, most pressing problem of the human race – not only of the human race, but of the whole of the biological kingdom from the beginnings of life... Thus we have been expressly evolved by nature – with all our impulses and deepest instincts – for the purpose of solving the economic problem."[13]

Keynes felt that the pursuit of wealth was not the problem, but rather the lack of deeper motivations. When he considered the optimistic prospect that mankind could decisively solve the "economic

---

[12] *The Meaning of Anxiety*, W.W. Nortor, 1977 (my italics)
[13] *Economic Possibilities for Our Grandchildren*, in The Nation and Athenaeum, 1930

problem," and what we might do with our newfound freedom from the pressing concerns of survival, he thought

> "with dread of the readjustment of the habits and instincts of the ordinary man, bred into him for countless generations, which he may be asked to discard... To use the language of today – must we not expect a general 'nervous breakdown'?"

Indeed, and nervous breakdown is what we have. The Sentinel does not retire once we have achieved some material comfort. While having *sufficient* money is important, surplus wealth fails to bring the happiness or sense of security we assume it will. Financial peace of mind does not translate into a mind at peace. Being loaded, it seems, is a low-calorie substitute that rarely satisfies real hunger. With fearful "habits and instincts" on autopilot, the Sentinel usurps the throne, and a sickness falls upon the land.

Dubbed "affluenza," it shows how neurosis seems to flourish in the soil of affluence. The term is defined as a "socially transmitted condition of overload, debt, anxiety, and waste, resulting from the dogged pursuit of more."[14] British psychologist Oliver James argues that the higher rates of mental and emotional challenges in consumerist cultures are a consequence of excessive wealth-seeking and its resultant inequality.[15] Prominent Australian economist Richard Denniss has asked: "If the economy has been doing so well, why are we not becoming happier?" He concludes that "luxury fever" leads to "psychological disorders, alienation and distress, provoking self-medication with mood-altering drugs and excessive alcohol consumption."[16]

These are the over-ripe fruits of the Atomic Age, when the worship of Wall Street culminated in the cocaine-fuelled orgy of Cold War consumerism that was the 1980s. Even today the dominant social ideology says that possession is the cure-all for discontent. Bombarded daily by countless ads that tell us acquisition brings joy, it is no surprise that we stay distracted from connecting to deeper priorities, and from finding the *intrinsic meaning* in our work. Meanwhile, the idea of gross national happiness is dismissed as a quaint notion for places like Bhutan.[17]

---

[14] *Affluenza: The All-Consuming Epidemic* by Graaf, Wann & Naylor. Berrett-Koehler, 2001
[15] *The Selfish Capitalist* by Oliver James. Vermilion, 2008
[16] *Affluenza: When Too Much Is Never Enough*, with Clive Hamilton. Allen & Unwin, 2005
[17] See www.grossnationalhappiness.com

Time Is Honey

A friend of mine was once set to marry the man of her dreams. They had just bought a beautiful property together, complete with sea views, and her life was clearly taking an upswing. Then, without explanation, her fiancé broke the engagement and got engaged to another woman two weeks later. Needless to say, she was devastated and disoriented. She found herself in a pit of despair.

A couple of months later, when I asked how she was feeling, she said she was doing alright, having been prescribed antidepressants. Perhaps it was not necessary to be OK yet, I tactfully suggested; it takes time to grieve and process hurt. But she had found herself too often at work under her desk crying. "I wasn't being productive," she said.

Without making any judgment on her chosen method for coping, I did find this exchange instructive. Under the influence of cultural conditioning, even internal distress and devastation cannot topple productivity from its plinth. After all, work is the great cure-all virtue. The good ol' Protestant work ethic has become so normalized, we hardly question it. But at what cost? The poet Emerson suggested: "Money often costs too much."

There is a clue to this question in our relationship to time. Judging from current hunter-gatherer cultures, for most of our history as a species, we regarded time as circular, not linear. That may seem odd or inconceivable, but even Einstein was on their side: "People like us who believe in physics know that the distinction between the past, the present and the future is only a stubbornly persistent illusion." For us in the industrialized world, however, time is no longer simply linear – we have also come to take it for granted that time is money.

"Wasting time" usually means not making money – being unproductive. Losing track of time is irresponsible. The clock is ticking, faster and faster, and our nervous systems had better get with the programme. But for most of our history, it was not this way.

In the Middle Ages, time was considered sacred. It was God-given, and therefore usury – the accumulation of interest – was considered a serious sin. Christian religious devotion had historically been accompanied by a rejection of mundane affairs, including economic pursuit. After 1600, however, Protestantism – notably Calvinism – supported the pursuit of economic gain and the worldly activities dedicated to it, seeing them as endowed with moral and spiritual significance. By the 18th century, the toiler and moralist Benjamin Franklin was reminding young men that "time is money." For Franklin and his ilk, the accumulation of money for its own sake became a virtue. They even painted it as a moral imperative. (Franklin is no doubt posthumously pleased to have his face on the hundred-dollar bill.)

From being a basic means of exchange, time married to money began to take on a life of its own. The medievals tried very hard to keep time and money separated for this very reason – they feared a corruption of the "brotherhood of man." For example, there are documented cases of rents remaining unchanged for 500 years.[18] Property was not bought and sold to make a profit, it was a culture of stewardship, and communes were encouraged and regarded as more important than making money. It has been estimated that in the 13th century, peasants in some European countries farmed their land about 150 days per year – a relaxed pace of life, working outdoors alongside friends and family. But with the Reformation, usury was absolved, and time and money were happily wed. It has been argued that this Protestant ethic was the very foundation for the Industrial Revolution.[19]

And it is a pre-industrial relationship with time that our souls and nervous systems are yearning to regain. For those hoping to end stress and anxiety, finding a more fulsome relationship to time is one of the challenges. Yeats captured this yearning beautifully in one of my favourite poems, *The Lake Isle of Innisfree*.

> I will arise and go now, and go to Innisfree,
> And a small cabin build there, of clay and wattles made;
> Nine bean rows will I have there, a hive for the honey bee,
> And live alone in the bee loud glade.
>
> And I shall have some peace there, for peace comes dropping slow,
> Dropping from the veils of the morning to where the cricket sings;
> There midnight's all a glimmer, and noon a purple glow,
> And evening full of the linnet's wings.
>
> I will arise and go now, for always night and day
> I hear lake water lapping with low sounds by the shore;
> While I stand on the roadway, or on the pavements grey,
> I hear it in the deep heart's core.

---

[18] *The Common Stream* by Rowland Parker. Academy Chicago Publishers, 1994
[19] *The Protestant Ethic and the Spirit of Capitalism* by Max Weber. Norton Critical Editions, 2009

When last did you have time for poetry, by the way? Well, many are making the time, and it has been given a name: "downshifting." Downshifting has become a social trend as a result of dissatisfaction with the consequences of the work-and-spend cycle and conditions in the workplace. Downshifters want a simpler life, opting out of the rat race. They reject obsessive consumerism and materialistic social status. It involves a voluntary reduction in income and spending. This might require taking an extra day or half-day off from work for leisure, or opting to work from home or in the local community. Often, though, downshifting requires only minor lifestyle changes. Whatever it looks like on an individual level, it is invariably motivated by a desire to reduce the stress and psychological expense that accompanies the dominant social ideology.

Downshifting is but one of several similar expressions of what Carl Honoré, in his book *In Praise of Slowness*, calls the global Slow Movement. Before this groundbreaking book, physicist Geir Berthelsen created the think-tank World Institute of Slowness, which put forth a vision for a "slow planet," and argued for the need to teach the world the way of slowness. Professor Guttorm Fløistad at the University of Oslo summarizes the values that are called for through a return to a moderate pace of life:

> "The only thing for certain is that everything changes. The rate of change increases. If you want to hang on you better speed up. That is the message of today. It could however be useful to remind everyone that our basic needs never change. The need to be seen and appreciated! It is the need to belong. The need for nearness and care, and for a little love! This is given only through slowness in human relations. In order to master changes, we have to recover slowness, reflection and togetherness. There we will find real renewal."

Counter-cultural movements help us think outside the box. How much of our lives is ruled by cultural conditioning? I've seen so many heroes of graft and captains of industry crash head-on into burnout, simply because they had blindly adopted the social programming and momentum of the money-mad world around them. Knowing more about the nervous system, and appreciating the historically unique pressures we now place ourselves under, and considering again the pace of life we were generally attuned to for most of our history, it is surprising *more* people are not burning out. It is not pathological, it is a perfectly healthy reaction!

To approach the true wealth of wellbeing, we have to think a little differently. We may have to relinquish the objective measures of our cultural value system – that virtue resides in working hard, and lucratively. These may be observable characteristics of a "good work ethic." But it is often founded on guilt and fear and the need for approval – insecurity.

To a large degree, the psychology underlying this insecurity, as well as the Puritan work ethic, seems to stem from something psychologists call "parental disapproval syndrome." This term refers to the psychological effects of relentless criticism and disapproval that gets passed from parent to child, generation to generation. It stems from the assumption that disapproving of things makes you a better person – the more you disapprove of, the more virtuous you are. It is easy to rationalize such an attitude as moral and responsible, because some degree of disapproval is obviously justified in life. But when parents adopt such an attitude as their default setting, children believe they always have to *earn* approval. And this becomes their working world – performing endless unpleasant activities, called "work," trying to quench the thirst for approval.

One must think differently to access work's subjective sense of *meaningfulness*. It is this sense of meaning, inspiration and depth that dictates access to the good life in the present. Keynes was asking: if we could put economic considerations aside, and if money was no longer a problem, what would we devote ourselves to then? Will we connect to larger perspectives and cultivate noble action, or will we keep running on habit; on a hamster wheel, mistaking motion for progress?

We can start by asking ourselves the question: is our work motivated by the survival instinct? Are we coasting on the momentum of mere busyness? Is our work fuelled by fear?

Take Care

I am not disparaging hard work. There is satisfaction in working hard. But often it is done for its own sake. Some say they function at their best when they are stressed, that they need that stress to motivate them to excellence. They call it "eustress" – euphorically stressed. What they really mean, I suspect, is that they like to feel challenged. It is inspiring to be engaged in a meaningful challenge. But when the challenges pile up and continue for too long, and especially when interpreted as meaningless, we get stressed. What develops is what is known as an "adrenalin addiction." As anyone who has worked for such a boss or team leader can attest, adrenalin addiction is disastrous for the healthy functioning of a company.

The problem presents itself when shallow motivations spur the work. Or worse, when whipping ourselves to pick up the pace in adherence to a puritanical idea of work ethic… when in fact, we are simply going through the motions; substituting productivity for creativity. The idea of the work ethic is a neurotic inheritance, and fails to question our notions of progress.

Ditch the work ethic – the world does not need it! Instead, discover work aesthetic – when labour resonates with goodness, truth and beauty. "Happiness is not in the mere possession of money," said Franklin D. Roosevelt. "It lies in the joy of achievement, in the thrill of creative effort." This joy of achievement requires us to be *effective*, not simply efficient. It requires a certain wakefulness and caring for any kind of work, even the most seemingly mundane. Shifting our perspective, so that we genuinely care, will burn brighter than any imposed work ethic.

I once sensed that a colleague disliked me. I later learnt that her assessment had been that I didn't care about the work. And she was absolutely right. During that particular freelance stint I was struggling with constant anxiety and my marriage was in trouble, so the last thing I cared about was the magazine I was working on, which was destined for the recycling heap anyway. What I failed to appreciate and respect was the loyal readership who found value in its pages. We were in fact making a contribution to the cultural narrative, and as a copy editor I was adding shine to a product with impactful content. There were stories about people overcoming adversity, and people devoting themselves to incredible causes. Stories of redemption, inspiration, rebirth. Stories of people wrestling the Angel of Fear, and finding a new and larger identity in surrender… It was all there, right in front of me, but I was so self-involved and obsessed with trying to feel better, that I failed to see it. I didn't care, when I had every reason to.

When work feels meaningless, Pan comes calling – if not with panic or anxiety, then perhaps with visions of early retirement to the countryside, or sipping sunset cocktails in a hammock on a beach. While those are, of course, lovely ideas, one must ask: are they good enough? In my own experience, when life lacks a sense of meaning or purpose, holidays can be hellish. Even while trying to relax, in the back of my mind I know that life's real work has yet to be done, and all I am doing is trying to escape – there is a difference between stress management and stress avoidance.

This sense of meaning is not measured objectively. It is rather the subjective sense that what you are engaged in has value. Caring is the key. Love is the essential ingredient. Like salt, the presence of love in an endeavour will bring out the flavour. In the words of the great Rumi:

> "Work is love made visible. And if you cannot work with love but only with distaste, it is better that you should leave your work and sit at the gate of the temple and take alms of those who work with joy. If you bake bread with indifference, you bake a bitter bread that feeds but half man's hunger."

It's an Adventure!

It is sad to see people subject themselves to toxic environments that slowly kill their spirit because they fear the consequences of taking a leap into the unknown.

After my recovery from anxiety, I became a full-time copy editor on the South African edition of O, *the Oprah Magazine*. I had been teaching a stress-reduction course at the Tibetan Kagyu Buddhist centre in Cape Town, and, having diligently practised meditation for some years, I became the daily mindfulness coach for Oprah's local online platform. I enjoyed my work, and found the structure grounding.

I went to the Company Gardens to meditate during lunch breaks, or took drives up to Deer Park to find Pan in the forest. During one such lunchtime walk, refreshed by mid-winter drizzle, I suddenly stopped in my tracks. A realization burst into awareness – "It's a trap!"

From the height of the mountain slopes, I looked down at the sprawling city and saw a wider vision for my life... I was too comfortable. Stagnant. I was surviving, not thriving. Although my work was enjoyable and good, I was not inspired, nor challenged – mostly semi-asleep. In that moment of clarity I knew it was time to wake up and seek a new horizon. I thought I would take stress-reduction and mindfulness to the working world... and to do so I would have to resign my job.

And then of course the fear kicked in. Quitting seemed madness – who turfs a decent job in a depressed economy? After all, I could pay the bills… at least I was safe. The "at leasts" gathered and gained weight. The consequences seemed foreboding – poverty, foreclosure, shame, homelessness, hunger, death. Six easy steps to final demise.

I returned to work after that enlightening walk excited and troubled in equal measure. Could I do the difficult thing, make the drastic change? I went to bed that night filled with doubt.

The next morning an unexpected staff meeting was called at the office. The editor, who had steered the magazine well for over a decade, had tears in her eyes. The owners of the publishing company were also there to inform us that, due to contract issues with the USA, they were dropping the magazine from their stable, and regretted to tell us that we were all retrenched.

Everyone spent the rest of that day in varying degrees of shock. No one had seen it coming. But I thought: thank God. I had not been sure that I could have worked up the courage, but now it was done. It felt like selfish synchronicity… like unseen hands were orchestrating events for my own growth. Yep, egocentric for sure.

The morning after our last day in the office, I received a call out of the blue. The founder of a dynamic company taking mindfulness into the corporate world had heard about me by word of mouth. In the year that followed, I found myself helping top executives and presenting lectures, and partnering with a Harvard-based institute. I travelled to the Caribbean and New York City with experiential workshops I had designed called Exploring Consciousness. I also launched my own company, End Stress (endstress.co.za).

Retrenchment was the best thing that could have happened to me!

I believe that the insight in the forest came to me from the inner spirit of Pan – the goat-god of adventure over routine. And adventure means going where we are not safe.

A Tibetan yogini said we should "go to the places that scare us." A literal interpretation of this injunction has seen monks and yogis spend nights meditating in graveyards. But perhaps there is a less literal suggestion here – that we take chances and choose directions that fly in the face of our fears.

While it felt as though my life had been given the kick it needed, and things had worked out remarkably well for me, I often wondered about my former colleagues, and whether they had found their feet. Two years later I ran into them, one by one, and in each case there was one of two possibilities – either they were as happy in their work as before, or that retrenchment had led to a remarkable transformation. I like to think there were more invisible hands at work than I had first imagined.

In the years since, I have spoken to many people about these work transitions, and I hear the same uncanny stories again and again. I'll risk seeming naïve, but I have come to wonder if we are subject to supernatural levels of help. Whether you want to call them angels, dakinis, guides or daemons, I simply observe that often we are too fortunate for it to just be luck. So often opportunities arise when we are willing to face fears, embrace change, and take a leap into the next evolution.

The biggest transformations came for my fellow copy editor. The typical bookish type. When I ran into him again, his slightly hunched walk had turned into a confident stride. His former pallid complexion now glowed, and his eyes were calm and crystal. He had hopped aboard *Men's Health* magazine, where he was forced to train in boxing. He and his wife were now devoted to super-healthy organic eating, and were planning to move to the country, where they would work remotely.

Another notable transformation was visible in one of the designers. She had taken unusual strain due to a difficult personality clash in her department at our offices. She had often been ashen-faced and mute with unhappiness, unable to resolve an unreasonable situation. It was painful to watch her natural joy drain away and her creativity stifled. She fretted because she could not take the leap – she felt that she was too old to find new work. Then I ran into her a year after the retrenchment. She was beaming, chatty and joyful, deeply satisfied in her new job, which gave her a sense of intrinsic meaning. She even looked younger. We spoke about how life had turned out, and she used the exact words.

"I sure am happy."

LET'S DO IT ♦ Improve the Company Culture

The most effective way to influence the "level of consciousness" is through our individual contribution to culture. Culture is our collective interior. Beneficial change must happen first in this domain, before we see a change in society or in organizational structures.

And so we might ask ourselves how we can influence the culture in our community or company for the better. "What is the culture of the company I work in? How can I creatively change or improve it?"

LET'S DO IT ♦ Find the Love in Your Work

Sometimes all it takes when work feels dry or a drudge, is to shift the perspective. Although this shift needs to go deep and become a permanent vantage point that brings inspiration, the following questions will help to get the shift started.

1. Who do you do your work for? Who does your work affect?

2. How is it meant to affect them? How are you benefitting them? How do their lives change and improve?

3. While recognizing the ripple effect you have on the world, whether you are an accountant, engineer, street sweeper or bureaucrat, ask yourself if there is any room for enhancing the benefit you provide to others. Can you make this tough world a better place through small, simple steps in your work life?

LET'S DO IT ♦ Proper Priorities

Death is a popular topic in contemplative traditions. Oddly, this does not result in a morbid attitude, but in growing happiness and resolve to do the things that matter. We think it will be far in the future, but we do not know. "Live," Nietzsche says, "as though the day were here."

1. Imagine you have one hour to live. Really imagine that this is the truth – try to feel it. Now in light of this awareness, reflect on your life. Have you done what you wanted to? Have you failed to do what you should have? What are you glad you have been able to achieve? What is most important? Earnestly engaging in this contemplation should bring your values into sharp focus.

2. Now imagine your doctor calls to say you have exactly one year to live. One year to do what is most important. You may not be able to travel around the world; you may have people depending on you. But how do you want to spend the next year making the most of your time? How can you best honour yourself, your soul's deepest yearnings, and the people you love?

9

RIDING LIONS

Entering their camp feels like slipping into a pool with sharks. The two teenaged cheetahs spiral closer, their dilated pupils sussing me for signs of stress.

"Just relax," says the animal trainer. "If you're tense they'll pick it up." Too late, I think. My nerves have ambushed me.

While preparing this trip for a newspaper piece on cheetah rehabilitation, I had imagined a cuddly bit of rough and tumble in the Karoo dust. Suddenly the prospect seems preposterous.

"What happens if they sense tension?" I ask.

"They might not let you pet them," she says, squatting down to greet the male face to face. She digs her fingers into his fur and a purr erupts like distant machine-gun fire. I'm relieved – at least the smell of fear doesn't automatically trigger a pounce, because I'm dripping in distress. These felines are technically tame, but only as tame as cheetahs get, which is still wild enough to ooze intimidation.

I lean over to touch the young female. She hisses at me and her beer-brown eyes turn to pools of black. I plaster myself to the fence. She slinks away.

"Don't worry," says the trainer. "She's a bit unsure with strangers. We're still building her confidence."

If anyone has a confidence problem it's me. I regret not being clad in chain mail. The cheetahs have the perky playfulness of kittens. But I know that kittens can get carried away – I recall my own cat's proclivity for climbing up my leg.

These cats have switchblades for thumbs. I walk around feigning calm and watch them while acting aloof. It's a bad strategy, as it allows just enough space for a run-up, and suddenly I'm on the receiving end of a frisky hug and bite. I nudge the male off and we both pad in opposite directions.

"Aw, he likes you," says the trainer. "He gave you a little love bite." She is straining not to laugh. "I'll take your word for it," I say and roll up my sleeve to admire the blood on my arm. Clearly another test of manhood down the tubes.

"It's best not to lean over them," she says. "If you kneel and position yourself to the side it's less threatening."

What I hear her say, is to surrender. Standing tall is a positional dominance. I'm set to fight. It also makes me mobile – ready for flight. As if I could beat a cheetah's velocity. I feel my reluctance to relinquish these paper-thin advantages. But I know what must be done: accept my fear, sit down and breathe.

Instead of kneeling as suggested, my meditation training accidentally kicks in, and I find myself in a half lotus position. Soles of my shoes facing up, back straight, hands resting in my lap. I'm not hunched in protection or coiled, ready to jump. I'm going nowhere. Surrendered but not defeated.

The trainer says nothing. I check in with myself. I recognise fear, and allow it. Why pretend? I make peace with the fear and forgive myself.

I'm not sure if I'm imagining it, but the cats seem calmer. The female strolls over and sits right in front of me. She pretends to ignore me at first, but, without thinking about it I simply lift my arm. She nudges her head against my hand.

The male comes closer too, and circles round to sit at my back. The trainer pets him, and there's that deep, primal purr vibrating into my spine. The most soothing sound in the universe.

To Be Or Not To Be

In my teens, the idea of meditation intrigued me enough to do my first silent Zen retreat. It was the most difficult and most rewarding thing I had ever done, and in the years that followed I was diligent and would regularly pretend to meditate.

After studying comparative religion at university, curiosity led me to a Buddhist seminary to become a novice monk at Nan Hua Temple, a satellite of the massive Fo Guang Shan organisation in Taiwan and part of the Pure Land sect of Chinese Buddhism. I thought this would make me awfully interesting. To girls, mostly. Just one catch — there were no girls in sight. I was sleeping on hardboard, getting up at 5am, shaving my head, the whole toot, and no one was in the least impressed.

It did not last but a seed was planted. A decade later, as I was trying to surrender to the Angel of Fear, I felt drawn to the meditation cushion again. Finding that acceptance helped dial down my anxiety, I wanted to learn *how* to accept. After all, it is far from easy to simply accept what feels intolerable.

This time I approached the practice from a different perspective. It was not a matter of curiosity anymore — it was do or die. I had no choice. The anxiety itself was already a 24/7 meditation master-class. A total, deep immersion in how not to fight my own thoughts and get tangled up in them. How to rest with whatever arises — including intense restlessness. How to be with my mauling mind. No wonder meditation is sometimes referred to as "taming the tiger."

Getting up close and personal with the cheetahs reminded me of a third-century member of my own ancestry — Saint Mamas. Semi-legend says he was tortured for his faith by the Roman emperor Aurelian. But an angel liberated him and led him to a cave in the mountains where he became a hermit. Later captured and thrown to the lions, he miraculously tamed them, in light of which he was set free. Afterwards, everywhere he went, he would be accompanied by one of these lions.

The lion-riding motif is not uncommon in religious iconography — another example is the Buddhist bodhisattva of wisdom, Manjushri. I feel this speaks to our relationship with fear. From the sabre-tooth to the African lion, the genus Panthera represents the prototypical predator. During most of human history, the big cats meant mortal danger. In iconography, however, they are not slain (conquered) or captured (controlled), but become vehicles of transformation.

And that is ultimately what mindfulness meditation is designed to do. With corporations taking to mindfulness, and secular mindfulness courses popping up everywhere, its origins are commonly ignored. It was not developed to increase productivity or lower blood pressure, but to achieve the transcendent, mystical mind of Awakening. Buddha, after all, means "awake."

What is meditation meant to help us wake up from? From the dream or nightmare of separate, isolated, egocentric existence. Meditation is meant to dissolve us into the transpersonal state of "enlightenment."

Whether you call it Big Mind, awakening, non-dual awareness, cosmic consciousness, nirvana, moksha, liberation or full realization, there is reportedly something called enlightenment – a state of consciousness radically different from our egocentric perspective, and one that is said to involve stepping out of a fundamental self-deception about our existence. Some eminently sane and serious people throughout history have attested to this experience.

There is one description of enlightenment I find particularly instructive – scholar Robert Thurman defines it as "the ultimate tolerance of cognitive dissonance." This again confirms that, when it comes to working with the mind, it is not our thoughts that matter, but the attitude with which we relate to these thoughts.

It is natural to oppose disturbing thoughts or feelings, and try to fight our way out of their clutches. But, as we have seen, we simply do not have that much control, and so, opposing them only creates conflict, which in turn keeps the mind in a state of disturbance.

In the method of mind training known as meditation, we learn to "let go" of our thoughts and feelings. And yet, even letting go of thoughts can have an undertone of rejection. "Letting be" is more accurate – we are giving ourselves a break from changing, fixing or sanitizing our minds. We do the radical thing: allow ourselves to just be an imperfect mess, and do nothing about it. Mindfulness meditation builds the courage, honesty and humility to face and accept ourselves as we are instead of how we think we ought to be. As the old Chinese proverb says: "Tension is who you think you should be. Relaxation is who you are."

So what is mindfulness? It is simply knowing what is happening, while it is happening, without preference. One could shorten that definition to: non-judgmental present-moment awareness.

Meditation is *not* about "emptying your mind" or "getting rid of thoughts." It is simply learning to let them be and gently bringing the focus back to the present moment. In this way we cultivate an attitude of unconditional acceptance toward our internal environment.

Through mindfulness the mind slowly becomes more stable, less wayward and reactive. But a stable mind is not the end goal – it is rather the necessary precondition for insight. As our mindfulness training progresses, we discover how reactive we are and how our minds are locked into habitual patterns and ways of thinking. Mindfulness eventually leads to a natural and spontaneous "seeing" into the workings of the mind. It shows us ever-deeper levels and what is going on beyond the limits of normal conscious awareness.

When we see into our conditioning and our neurotic complexes, we are freed from their unseen influence over our behaviour. The Tibetan word for meditation is *gom*, which means "to become familiar with." Becoming familiar with our minds, we eventually see through its tricks and self-deceptions. This insight liberates us from the mental torture we cause ourselves. It is an ongoing process or "path," until the complex that is the ego is seen through completely. Meditation teacher Chögyam Trungpa said: "Enlightenment is ego's ultimate disappointment."

The first stage of mindfulness training leads to the development of tranquillity – but not because we struggle to become tranquil. Simply let everything be as it is, and slowly the mind becomes tranquil all by itself, without interference. Distraction – a common problem – slowly subsides and peace of mind and relaxation in the moment becomes possible.

Before tranquillity comes, however, this path toward ultimate sanity may have to lead right into the middle of the muck and murk of our natural madness. To step out of self-deception, we must first see and accept that we are in it. When we bring unseen agendas to the practice – hoping to improve or purify, transcend or sanitize our minds – these preferences easily distort what is actually there. This is why an attitude of compassionate self-acceptance is crucial for clear seeing.

After starting mindfulness practice, it may feel as though our mental chaos is increasing. Actually, we are simply beginning to see the chaos that was always there – the notorious monkey mind. They say talking to yourself out loud is a sign of madness – well, we may not be doing it out loud, but we are talking to ourselves all the time, and in our heads it can get pretty loud. Woody Allen's films are perfect portraits of what the Buddhists call "samsara" – the normal state of mind, which literally translates as "going around in circles." Cate Blanchett's mad mumbling in *Blue Jasmine*, is simply an amplification of the everyday mind. Meditation eventually helps turn down the volume, but the complaint that "things are getting worse" is often heard when people start practising meditation. The fact is, they are simply becoming more aware of the relentless distraction that has always been present.

The subliminal mind courses like an underground river below the surface mind of discursive thought. It is accessible to fine-tuned awareness, but mostly remains unseen. An egocentric preference system is hard at work in the subliminal. It's an over-eager mechanism, meeting sounds and flavours and sights with a constant stream of judgment. When you boil it down, preference is what drives stress.

The mindful attitude of non-judgment or acceptance relaxes this grip of egocentric preference. Cultivating this internal attitude of acceptance and compassion is not navel-gazing – it literally changes the world.

When we first start sitting down to meditate, there is often a subtle sense of waiting for something to happen, as if we expect we should enter a feel-good trance. Actually we are training to come out of the trance we are already in most of the time – the "lost in thought" trance. Initially we might expect mindfulness to bring only preferred mind states, like peace or bliss. This makes us marinate in a sense of failure when tranquillity eludes us. True meditation involves giving up the struggle to achieve "spiritual" states.

Meditation helps make us more real, more authentic, more ourselves. The prism of our unseen assumptions and expectations often distort the experience of the present moment. That is why, once we sit down to practise, it is good to remind ourselves that the job is done, and now we can just relax with whatever may come up. Meditation is not trying to be a better person, nor to achieve bliss or tranquillity. It is simply creating the space in which to expose and undo our neuroses, self-deceptions and hidden hopes and fears.

No wonder we have these hidden fears – we spend so much time living in the future. "I can handle this moment, but the next may be my downfall," says fear. When we linger in the present, we stop feeding fear. When I was with the cheetahs, I was able to accept my inner reactions and allow the situation to be beyond my control; to sit down and be mindfully present. And the cats calmed down by themselves. I had been obsessed with how tame they were, because I wanted control.

In meditation, we don't tame the tiger. The tiger tames itself.

THE SEVENTH CONSCIOUSNESS

The image of saints and bodhisattvas riding lions suggests a taming of the wild mind, and a transformation of the relationship to fear – the skill to ride fear, instead of running or fighting. It also evokes a synergy between nature, red in tooth and claw, and transcendent awareness. Have we not seen a similar configuration before – human above, animal below?

In Chapter 7 we met the god Pan. But there is still more to the goat-god – his dual nature. Pan is both regressive *and* transcendent. He plays the panpipes, which sound both natural and ethereal. He is rooted in the earth and the instincts, an animal from the waist down, but also welcome and beloved on Mount Olympus. Pan is both pre-rational, and trans-rational. The head and heart in harmony.

As part of the process of spiritual growth, transpersonal psychologist Michael Washburn calls most dark nights of the soul, like periods of depression or anxiety, "regression in the service of transcendence." Pan represents precisely this, and I have come to believe that there may also be a transcendent core to the experience of panic.

During intensive meditation practice, it is not uncommon to experience powerful bursts of fear. Rather than rush to judgment that something has gone terribly wrong, this can be celebrated as a good sign. Because, on meditation retreats, we approach transpersonal states of consciousness, where the personal sense of self either falls away briefly, or teeters on the brink of self-extinction. What the Buddhists call the seventh consciousness, the fundamental sense of having or being a "self," collapses. Initially this may happen for only an instant – but then the self, sensing its own destruction, gets a shock and reasserts its dominion in a flash, countering with an overwhelming fear of annihilation. This is "panic as a destructively sublime communion with the Infinite."[20]

Lingering on that border, between a deep release into the unknown, and a fearful self-contraction, can actually be fun. Not much gets written about these less-than-pleasant experiences in meditation literature, most likely because experienced meditators know it is not a problem, and prefer not to deter anyone from the practice.

In Buddhism, the sense of self is something of a paper tiger – it is not real in the way that we feel it to be real. It is not static, nor self-existing. We have no unchanging essence. The Buddha called this *anatta* – no-self. Whenever we approach an experience of, or direct insight into, no-self, it is only natural that panic comes to preserve the self's conviction in its own existence.

When I travelled to India to meet one of Tibetan Buddhism's great teachers, the 12th Tai Situpa, I saw someone living beyond the sense of self. He inhabits a consciousness expanded beyond the limitations that constrict most of us. From our perspective, this may seem like an altered state of consciousness, but from the point of view of the "enlightened" mind, ours is the altered state of consciousness. This is why enlightenment is often called the "natural mind."

---

[20] *After the Orgy* by Dominic Pettman. SUNY Press, 2002

The Tai Situpa counselled me: "Enjoy your nightmares. There's no such thing as fear." On the one hand, this statement seemed nonsensical... and yet in the moment he said it, I felt it was true. I did not have to understand it conceptually for it to make sense. A statement like this may not seem rational, but just because it is non-rational, does not make it irrational. There is a distinction between truths that are trans-rational, and delusions that are pre-rational. I would classify this statement from the Tai Situpa as a trans-rational truth. Because although we obviously experience fear, and therefore there *is* such a thing as fear, when the illusory sense of self is extinguished (which is what the word *nirvana* means), then there is no longer any fear, for there is no longer any self to protect – and there never really was.

My theory is that many initial panic attacks contain the seed of the mystical impulse toward transcendence. It could be that, during deep fatigue, following a prolonged period of stress, the psychological energy to keep the sense of self propped up and firmly in place, simply bottoms out for a moment. But before the ego reaches full dissolution and a mystical awakening occurs, panic erupts as the emergency reserve kicks in – like a generator to ensure that the show goes on. There is, after all, a convenient self-obsession that follows in panic's wake.

Rest assured it usually takes extraordinary amounts of meditation on retreat to encounter these tricky experiences. While they can certainly be very strong, I no longer mind, and take it as a sign that I am drifting in the right direction. Meditation itself builds the capacity to not mind what arises in meditation.

Taming the tiger does not mean ridding ourselves of fear, but rather riding fear. Instead of fighting or running from the lion, get right up close, on its back, and become familiar with it. Let it carry you toward transformation.

At times during spiritual or psychological expansion, it feels like you are in freefall, disoriented and without conceptual bearings or reliable reference points. There is an ambivalence, the flavour of uncertainty or confusion. Like you are off the map. But the fact is, these are the hallmarks of transformation. The deck is being reshuffled. The king is dead. Long live the king. And yet again, off with his head.

MIND TO THE BODY

In the early years of the Vietnam War, an American platoon was hunkered down in a rice paddy, engaged in a fierce battle with the

Vietcong. Suddenly six monks appeared out of the forest and, on a buttress separating paddy from paddy, walked directly toward the line of fire. Without looking up or slowing down, they approached the hail of bullets. The shooting stopped and the monks passed between the warring groups. After they disappeared into the forest, there was only silence. "The fight just went out of us," recounts platoon member David Busch. "I just didn't feel like doing this anymore." The Americans and Vietcong both retreated, in silent accord. There would be no more fighting that day.

This incident dramatically demonstrates the potential power of mindfulness, and the ripple effect it can have on those around us. Our mere presence, our being – who we are, rather than what we are or what we do – has an enormous effect. Those monks did not achieve anything through their doing, but rather through their *being*.

Our souls cry out for us to be human *beings*, while instead we become human *doings*, acting on compulsion and autopilot. As the mythologist Joseph Campbell said: "We're so engaged in doing things to achieve purposes of outer value that we forget that the inner value, the rapture associated with being alive, is what it's all about."

We must learn being, and learn it well – wellbeing. This is foremost a *physical* experience. And although we are sitting still and working with the mind, meditation is essentially an *embodied* practice.

The movement from the mind to the body seems a crucial ingredient to many spiritual paths and healing protocols, but in the intellectualized complexity of our modern culture, overdosed on information, this can be a challenge. Our reflexive tendency to conceptualize is so ingrained, the philosopher Foucault went so far as to claim that modern man is almost incapable of even sexual experience without mediating it through his mind – that we have sex in our heads, not in our bodies. "Behind your thoughts and feelings, my brother," says Nietzsche, "there stands a mighty ruler, an unknown sage – whose name is self. In your body he dwells; he is your body."

"Body on your seat, mind in your body, mind in relaxation." Thus the 19th-century Tibetan teacher and "enlightened vagabond" Patrul Rinpoche summed up meditation: bringing the body to the cushion; bringing the mind to the body; bringing ease to the whole endeavour.

Bringing the mind to the body sounds simple, but it is one of the most significant things we can do to increase mindfulness and decrease stress and anxiety. Why? Because the body is planted in the present moment. While the mind is usually lost in fantasies of the future or memories of the past, the body is our immediate access to now. This is why the breath is most often used as a focus during meditation. Similarly, one of the most effective preliminary practices for meditation is the "body scan," where we systematically bring attention to different parts of the body.

The Buddha himself was quite emphatic on the importance of the body. In the *Satipatthana Sutta* he says:

> "There is one thing that, when cultivated and regularly practiced, leads to deep spiritual intention, to peace, to mindfulness and clear comprehension, to vision and knowledge, to a happy life here and now, and to the culmination of wisdom and awakening. And what is that one thing? It is mindfulness centred on the body."

Because fear feeds on ruminations about the future, when we linger in the present, we stop feeding fear. We have also seen in Chapter 4 how the neurological odds are stacked against us when we wish to control our feelings. When the limbic brain is activated, the rational neocortex simply does not have adequate synaptic access to override emotions that are running high. But thankfully there is a far more effective way to access the limbic brain – through the body. The limbic brain and the body are intertwined. The limbic brain, ironically, is more intimate with the body than it is with the rest of the brain.

For this reason, I place a strong emphasis on acceptance-based physical techniques in my workshops. By working with the body, we give soothing signals to the over-activated limbic brain. With repeated practice of any physical techniques designed to bring the nervous system back into balance, their cumulative effect – over time – down-regulates the HPA-axis (see Chapter 4).

While bringing the mind to the body through meditation halts fearful rumination, in the case of severe anxiety it is sometimes more helpful to first prep the nervous system for a few weeks or months with relaxation techniques that are more physical. One example of such a technique is what I like to call the old faithful – progressive muscle relaxation (PMR). It remains one of the most effective ways to trigger the body's natural relaxation response.

American physician Edmund Jacobson developed PMR during his research into psychosomatic "disorders" in the 1920s. His major work was a book addressing the general public with the beautifully old-school title *You Must Relax*. However, it was the world-renowned and award-winning South African psychologist Joseph Wolpe who used the technique to revolutionize the field of behavioural therapy.

Enlisted in the South African Army as a medical officer during the Second World War, Wolpe worked with soldiers with post-traumatic stress, at that time called "war neurosis." The mainstream treatment for soldiers was drug therapy, in which a "truth serum" prompted soldiers to talk about their experiences. Once a dedicated follower of Freud, Wolpe was disturbed to discover that talk therapy was simply not effective. A lack of successful treatment outcomes forced him to question psychoanalytic therapy and search for more effective options.

The result was "systematic desensitization," which would provide several generations of clinicians with their most potent natural technique for working with severe anxiety. PTSD patients were taught how to relax each of the body's major muscle groups, and were then slowly coached to recall their traumatic memories. Over time, they would progressively learn to associate these anxiety-provoking images with a relaxation response, thereby reconditioning their nervous systems to be able to integrate the disturbing memories. For Wolpe, the key to overcoming fears was "by degrees."

Try the PMR exercise on my free *Still Life* album, at *albertbuhr.com*.

SHAKEN, NOT STIRRED

When swimming in shark-infested waters, I have taken solace in the knowledge that I do not need to swim faster than an approaching fin – I only need to swim faster than the chap next to me.

Antelope must surely share this overconfidence. When a cheetah takes chase, a springbok just doesn't want to be in the bronze category. But this is not the only reason animals in the wild who escape the mortal maw rarely exhibit symptoms of trauma – they also have recourse to something called "neurogenic tremoring."

When an animal singled out by the fastest predator on land somehow manages to survive, it will pass through a phase of visible tremors once it is safe again. From the outside it might look like the poor thing is so shaken it is about to go to pieces, but in fact it is simply exhibiting a natural biological response to bring the autonomic nervous system back into balance.

These tremors are an innate adaptive response to stress that humans share with other mammals in the wild. Research on the effects of tremors in humans after a traumatic episode has corroborated the findings in animal research – neurogenic tremors in humans is the natural response of a shocked or disrupted nervous system attempting to restore its balance. It allows the nervous system to "thaw out" the freeze response.

As humans, we have managed to remove ourselves from nature to such a degree, and to ignore our instincts and control our impulses so successfully, that this adaptive response is well repressed. Our modern conditioned response maintains a state of tension, which can accumulate over time to create anxiety while nervous energy rarely gets to discharge. It seems that, as a species, we have been socialized out of this natural response through the egocentric association between trembling and weakness or loss of control. Occasionally, however, when we are subjected to an extreme shock, our bodies will automatically override our repression and start tremoring.

It is well documented that neurogenic tremors are a common result of a traumatic event, and are also recognized as diagnostic features in PTSD, panic attacks, social phobias and other anxieties. By harnessing these instinctual tremors instead of treating them as pathology, humans, like animals, can resolve the physical expressions of their trauma and restore the natural balance in the autonomic nervous system.

It is exciting news – we can discharge this energy trapped in the nervous system, by inducing neurogenic tremors through exercises that fatigue the iliopsoas muscles. Following his experiences as a volunteer in various war zones around the world, Dr David Berceli was the first to develop a set of effective exercises to induce these tremors, which he calls Trauma Release Exercises (TRE). I have worked out a different series of exercises that suit me better, but the effect is the same – fatigue in the iliopsoas triggers the autonomic nervous system to initiate a rebalancing discharge. The tremors originate in the limbic circuitry, and are meant to discharge the unused energy that is activated by the sympathetic nervous system (the accelerator). It allows the fight-or-flight response to run to completion, and thereby restore homeostasis or balance, while also releasing deep muscle tensions at the physical core.

Even though induced tremors are generally gentle, the feeling can be a little uncanny at first, because they are partly involuntary. One of my workshop participants confessed great discomfort when I taught her how to induce the tremors. When I questioned her, we both soon realized the discomfort was not physical, but emotional – she hated not being in control. I simply showed her how to stop the tremors by changing position. Some weeks later she had a severe fall while hiking in the mountain, and fractured her hip in several places. While waiting for the rescue helicopter to airlift her out, her body started to tremor quite intensely, and in that moment she was finally able to accept the process and welcome it as a natural and beneficial reaction. She had to work hard to reassure her partner, who reportedly was more concerned about the tremors than the fall! She made a speedy recovery, and was training to run marathons just months later.

These tremors also seem to commonly occur after surgery, but because the understanding of neurogenic tremoring is not yet adequately studied or understood, doctors routinely block them with strong medication.

It is not sufficient to learn the exercises from a book – one needs to be trained by an experienced guide. Bercelli's work has a global reach, and you are likely to find a TRE practitioner near you through an easy online search. Anecdotal evidence is showing this technique to be highly effective, from refugees to war veterans. Yet, you don't need to have experienced violent trauma to benefit. It also seems to work on the general accumulation of stress, and "the heartache and the thousand natural shocks that flesh is heir to."

Tension gets locked into the iliopsoas (or simply psoas, for short), because while we instinctively want to curl into a ball when we experience trauma or are overwhelmed, we rarely allow ourselves to do so, and rather override this instinct, possibly due to enculturation. This movement known as "flexor withdrawal" then never comes to completion. An accumulation of tension results. Muscle tissues can become as hard as biltong (beef jerky), as many a masseuse will attest. The problem is that the psoas is situated so deep within our bodies, that it is mostly inaccessible through therapeutic massage.

We use the psoas to bend at the waist in order to take the foetal position – a natural defensive instinct. It is our core muscle, and it is richly supplied by the nerve fibres of the autonomic nervous system. It even affects our ability to breathe. The healthy functioning of the psoas is intimately tied to overall health and vitality, as well as our ability to cope with stress.

Trauma tends to cause a degree of dissociation from the body. Many of us live some distance away from our bodies, whether through excessive rumination, conceptualization, or basic unawareness. In my opinion, anxiety's many strange physical symptoms are calling us back into our bodies. Through these symptoms the Angel of Fear seeks to remind us to be *embodied*. A signpost for this is the motif where man and animal meld – the centaur, the goat-god, the mystic riding the lion. It is the call to healing the split between our bodies and our minds – the essence of mindfulness. It is, very simply, the call to *being*.

LET'S DO IT ♦ Rest the Mind

Although it is always best eventually to find a good meditation teacher, there is no reason not to start meditating right away. In the beginning, even 5 or 10 minutes is good – any amount of time spent has been shown to affect the brain's ability to change itself, thanks to the phenomenon known as neuroplasticity. The more you do, the more you decrease the density of the amygdala, where fear and anxiety register, and thicken the prefrontal cortex, which is the physical seat of self-awareness. These effects can be seen with fMRI brain scans within weeks. Meditation works! And anyone can do it.

Follow this formula for beginning your meditation practice of mindfulness of the breath.

1. Body on Your Seat
Sit down in a posture that is comfortable yet attentive, and set your intention:
a) to benefit yourself (by resting the mind in the present moment and letting go of fantasies and inner commentary)
b) to better benefit other people (through your growing capacity for true presence)
c) and to do all that by simply returning your attention to the support (breath) over and over again.

2. Mind in Your Body
For several minutes, place your awareness in your body. Make adjustments to your posture until you find a good balance, so that you are not straining any muscles to stay upright. There is no such thing as the "perfect posture," so simply find what works best for you, and what position is most conducive to both ease and focus – reclining, for example, usually leads to a sleepy dullness, so it is better to sit up. Then continue to scan your body for any tensions, and relax. Once the body begins to feel settled, see if you can recognize the subtle physical pleasure in complete stillness.

3. Mind at Ease
Now invite your awareness to the sensation of breathing. When you notice you have engaged with thinking, relax and return to the breath. Do this very gently. Do not make a problem of your mind wandering, it is perfectly natural. Return to the breath over and over, and let thoughts and feelings be as they are. As you inhale, let the fresh air relax you from

inside, and as you exhale, cultivate the feeling of *letting go*. Hold your attention to the breath as light as you would hold an angel's feather...

LET'S DO IT ♦ Mindful Driving

Many of us spend hours each week driving, and we have an important choice to make – we can either spend that time hardwiring our brains for stress, or practising mindfulness that leads to tranquillity. In traffic, we may easily find ourselves deep into a stress response and reactivity – which indicates prime time for hardcore mindfulness practice. So buckle up and try these mindful driving strategies.

1. Tether your attention to your body

You can use the breath, or perhaps try the sensation of your hands on the steering wheel. Your hands are in a position to command your attention while not distracting from the road in front of you. This technique trains your capacity for "open focus." This body-based focal point acts as a present-moment reference from which to recognize the wandering mind, thereby also training your attention in the face of outer distraction as you navigate the way to your destination. It also helps you to develop a panoramic awareness around the point of focus, encouraging an "open" quality to your focus.

2. Go with the flow

The prerequisite for this part of mindful driving is to never be late or in a hurry! Always prepare your travels with time to spare. Five minutes late tends to have a much steeper price than five minutes early. Eckhart Tolle defines stress as "being here but wanting to be there." Nowhere is this more obvious than when trying to get somewhere in a car when you are late and everyone is in your way...

Now, assuming you do not have to rush, return your attention repeatedly to your hands on the steering wheel (or your breath), sense the natural flow of the traffic, and come into harmony with it. When overtaking, do it in a measured way that accords with the momentum of the cars around you.

Float like a butterfly... and in time you will learn that, whether you drive like a speed demon or a near-sighted granny, you will probably get to your destination with very little time difference. Why? Because traffic lights are great equalizers. For the price of three or four minutes, you will gain a sense of time as abundant, and that is priceless.

3. Create mindfulness triggers

When you get into the car, decide on mental triggers for mindfulness. For example, a red light is the perfect mindfulness trigger. It is saying: stop; slow down; take a pause. It is the perfect reminder to come back to your body and recognize the urge to be elsewhere. While waiting for the light to change, split your attention between the redness of the light while coming back to the sensation of breathing. Notice how you might be conditioned to dislike the red light, and try to see it in a new light… the cherry-red luminosity is actually beautiful.

4. Leave anger at the kerb

The car ahead of you signals to turn left, but moments later, turns right. A minor incident, but one you react to by swearing and blaring your horn. Why? Because the brain is doing a lot of work, making countless decisions while drawing on over a thousand psychomotor skills to get you from point A to point B. To curb that stress response, try this mindful driving game: give the first five drivers *the right to be wrong* – to make a mistake while driving. After car number five, you can vent all you want. You may discover that the others after that don't have much effect on you.

10

COMPASSION CURES

Playing guitar under water in the open ocean while a great white circles closer might seem mad on multiple levels. But for Andy Brandy Casagrande IV, it's no big deal.

Shark Angel Andy, as he has been dubbed for his contributions to conservation, was born in New York and first became fascinated with sharks after seeing a TV documentary as a young boy. After college he worked at a software company, which left him bored and dissatisfied. While sitting at his desk he spent every chance he got to learn more about sharks and where he could find them.

One day he mailed a recording of a shark-themed song he composed to a research team in Cape Town. They were so amused they invited him to join them as a volunteer. In the following two years he worked part-time on fishing vessels off the US East Coast to gain experience and fund his volunteer work in Cape Town. After experimenting with underwater cameras, National Geographic noticed his enthusiasm and offered him a job, eventually sending him all over the world on wildlife adventures. Just a few years later, he won an Emmy for Outstanding Cinematography.

I met Andy while writing a newspaper article on sharks and we quickly became friends. "I don't get that freaked out really," he says, "but it is funny how I will be out there actually swimming with a great white while the host, who is in a cage, makes this huge deal about how dangerous they are and how they'll eat you in one second." Andy eventually filmed a music video of the song that first took him to Cape Town, which changed his life. The Great White Shark Song can be seen on YouTube, and shows a large shark lurking as Andy strums his guitar. Its comedic lyrics, as well as Andy's answers when pressed on the issue of swimming unprotected, reveal his natural inclination to take the shark's point of view. His palpable empathy for these creatures is stronger than his panic.

It is said sharks can sense fear, which may make them more likely to attack. If there is truth to that, my body would be a dinner bell. How does Andy not let fear overtake him? The opposite of anxiety is not calm, but compassion. A deep and genuine love quells Andy's fear. Caring acceptance creates the calm that keeps him safe.

THE SACRED HEART

In the first chapter I suggested a reflection called Fear-free Me. I asked you to consider what your life would be like without the influence of fear. This is worth consideration, because in fact, absolute fearlessness is our human potential.

Where there is the thought of *me*, there is fear. Essentially, there is no "fear-free me." Our basic sense of self is entwined with fear. And the way to lessen fear, is "letting go of oneself."

Although the experience is rare, it is possible to let go all the way to a certain threshold, beyond which the *me* subsides completely. When this happens, it feels like the weight of the world is lifted off one's shoulders. Only then do we even realize we have been carrying that crushing weight. The feeling is much like waking up from a bad dream. The sense of relief is cosmic.

In the Buddhist tradition this rare and hard-won experience is sometimes called *the deathless*. The fear of death evaporates, because death is recognized as an illusion. But of course, we do all die, so is this just pre-rational wishful thinking or spiritual babble? No, because the one that recognizes the illusion of death is no longer *me*. The *me* dies… but there is something more that remains. Waking up from the wheel of life and death also means waking up from the dream of *me*.

Our collective "crisis of fear," as the psychologist and cultural critic Erich Neumann called it, is the consequence of a failure to evolve beyond the narrow notions of ourselves. The expansion of consciousness I have referred to entails a process of dropping the barriers that make up the borders of *me*. Not only of transcending, but also of including – becoming ever more whole, by re-integrating cut-off, natural parts of ourselves.

As consciousness expands in this way, we gain the ability to take on a growing number of perspectives. We feel what it is like to walk in others' shoes. We can even appreciate a shark's perspective, and learn to love a creature we had once thought of as terrifying.

Anxiety, neurosis, is the traction of resistance to this expansion. It is the chafe. Expansion rarely occurs without a struggle. While the psyche promotes growth, it is also conflicted – it is loath to give up what it knows. But this process of growth – so often against our will – is not only an expansion of consciousness but also an expansion of heart. The poet Rumi says: "Your task is not to seek for love, but merely to seek and find all the barriers within yourself that you have built against it." We have built those barriers because we fear the heart will compromise us. Or even tear us apart – we fear drowning in an ocean of primitive impulse. And so, as we learn to "use our words," we learn to suppress.

Through suppression, we cobble together an identity, a sense of self in relation to others – family, friends, tribe. We then pretend that this identity project is more than a construct teetering towards collapse when challenged. We convince ourselves and others that it is a thing of substance – real and to be respected. "Look at me" it says. "If you don't love me, you must fear me." And as this rickety self rises, it casts a shadow where all the self-judgments hide.

This is the cauldron of classic narcissism – a seething stew of excessive interest in one's own self, one's own abilities and importance. And not only that, but others must be diminished. It is egocentrism stuck in arrested development. Most psychologists agree that narcissism is a normal trait of childhood that is outgrown more and more as we develop. In fact, human development has been defined as a *successive decrease in egocentrism*.[21] Collectively and individually, we grow from egocentric through ethnocentric consciousness, to world-centric and eventually cosmic consciousness. This ever-expanding spiral is defined by an increase in acceptance, care and compassion. And as egocentricity decreases, empathy fills the space once occupied by *me*.

I have said that anxiety, far from being a psychiatric illness, is a call to transformation. Anxiety makes self-fixation so painful that we finally have no other option but to let go of ourselves and our self-protection, and open our hearts in surrender.

This is the great gift of the Angel of Fear.

---

[21] *Frames of Mind* by Howard Gardner. 1983. *A Theory of Everything* by Ken Wilber. 2001

Embracing the Feminine

Surrender is a Feminine quality and, whether we are male of female, to reduce stress and anxiety we often need to embrace the inner Feminine. This is of course not to devalue the Masculine, but simply to redress the imbalance of a patriarchal consciousness, under which men also suffer. Whether we call it Masculine or Feminine, Yang or Yin, sympathetic or parasympathetic, accelerator or brake, the aim is balance.

Erich Neumann was much concerned about the one-sidedness of patriarchal Western civilization. He believed that balancing the Feminine and the Masculine in both the individual and collective psyche is one of our fundamental tasks. In *Fear of the Feminine* he writes:

> "The consequence of the patriarchal male's haughtiness toward women leads to the inability to make any genuine contact with the Feminine, i.e., not only in a real woman but also with the Feminine in himself, the unconscious. Whenever an integral relationship to the Feminine remains undeveloped, however, this means that, due to his fear, the male is unable to break through to his own wholeness that also embraces the Feminine. Thus the patriarchal culture's separation from the Feminine and from the unconscious becomes one of the essential causes for the crisis of fear in which the patriarchal world now finds itself."

To redress this imbalance, we must turn inwards, and take seriously our inner lives and the needs of the soul. While nature and art facilitate this movement, another way to do this is through the "royal road to the unconscious" – our night-time dreams. Taking an interest in our dreams, and keeping a dream journal, however basic, creates a bridge to the unconscious.

"Inner life is pale and ephemeral when the ego does not turn to it, believe in it, and endow it with reality," says James Hillman. "This investment, this commitment to inner life, increases its importance and gives it substance." He continues to explain how "a new feeling of self-forgiveness and self-acceptance begins to spread and circulate. It is as if the heart were extending its dominion."

Through keeping a dream journal, we establish a dialogue with soul. The ancient Greeks referred to soul as Psyche – a goddess that suggests that our inner, imaginal world is essentially Feminine. This is represented in the archetype of the "anima." When someone is full of life, we say they are "animated." Without this connection to the anima, we may feel dull and listless. Today we call this depression, but in ancient cultures it was known as a loss of soul. For Jung and Hillman, this development of the inner Feminine – or anima development – was of primary importance. In broad terms, it entails opening up to emotionality and a deepening spirituality that includes the imagination and sensitivity to the inner lives of ourselves and others.

This is the terrain of soul, defined by depth. Soul gives necessary ballast to spiritual pursuit. Expanding consciousness is not just about climbing the mast towards the heights of spirit and sky, but also about braving the hold, down in the bottom of the boat, submerged, where the cannons are stored during storms. Down below is where the pirates keep their treasure.

Dreams take us down into the hold and invite us to spend time with the treasures there. Thomas Moore describes it well in his book *The Soul's Religion*: "Dreams often connect heaven and earth and heal the rift we usually feel between our transcendent lives and the depth of our emotions and life progress. While we are attending to dreams the focus shifts and the very *sense of self* broadens and deepens."

The soul expresses itself in images, and care of the soul requires that we pay attention to these images, but with a receptive Feminine attitude, rather than an egoic analysis. My dream journal functions to relax the urgency to know everything and be in control. Recording my dreams teaches me to become comfortable with mystery. "All dreams reveal spiritual experience, provided one does not apply one's own point of view to the interpretation of them," says Jung. In his book *The Dream and the Underworld*, Hillman further recommends letting a dream take us down into the unknown rather than trying to decipher or explain it. And as Thomas Moore says: "The important thing is not what you do to a dream but what the dream does to you." In this way, engaging with our dreams cultivates our inner Feminine capacities.

Another way to access the Feminine, is through one of our body's most remarkable hormones. Biochemistry explains much of why men and women seem to handle stress very differently. In women, a good dose of the famous love hormone oxytocin gets released from the brain in response to heightened stress chemicals like cortisol and adrenalin, effectively encouraging the instinct to *relate*. It has also been called the "cuddle chemical," and is part of a woman's natural tendency toward tending and nurturing. Men are not so lucky. When cortisol rises in men, there is almost no release of oxytocin. Men are from Mars, remember?

Oxytocin would just scupper our capacities for war.

When the fight-or-flight response is triggered, some men sadly indulge the destructive impulse to fight, whether verbally or physically. Most, however, tend to listen to the angels of their better nature and choose flight – they escape, run away, hide. We need our man caves. In response to stress, men prefer to play golf, or watch sport, or more questionable attempts at changing the biochemical landscape, like drinking or pornography. Without the same release of oxytocin, men seek to distract themselves. This is often done in unhealthy ways that are self-defeating and result in a loss of vital energy. While women's natural tendency is to seek support, and to talk out the emotional experience, to process what is happening and what might be done, men turn to stone instead.

A recent study published in the journal *NeuroReport* indicates that, under acute stress, men have less brain response to facial expressions. Next to women, one could almost call men ill-equipped to interpret emotions in others. Mara Mather, the study's lead author and director of the Emotion and Cognition Lab at the University of Southern California, points out that "women showed the opposite – women under stress had increased activity in the regions of the brain used in interpreting facial emotions."

It is no wonder that women tend to outlive men – whereas women seek connection as a response to stress, men are far more likely to repress their feelings and go into denial. Men can subconsciously equate emotional distress with weakness, so they try to hide it. The overwhelming majority of my course participants have been women, and I doubt this is because women are any more susceptible to stress. I believe men just have the added burden of (imagined) shame to contend with. Men are far more likely to withdraw socially and indulge in unhealthy habits. This creates something of a pressure cooker, and only adds to the stress.

So what is the solution? Oxytocin, of course. The bumper stickers were right: love is the answer. This bonding hormone has an unusually long list of benefits, but most importantly it protects the vagus nerve – the trunk of the parasympathetic nervous system (the brake). It offers some of the best stress-busting bang for your buck.

Oxytocin is the brain's direct and immediate antidote to cortisol. It down-regulates the HPA-axis and lowers cortisol immediately. That is why, when a child or friend is upset, our natural inclination is to hug or hold them. Neuroscientists are discovering that any time we feel valued and loved, a dose of oxytocin is activated in the brain.

For many men, doing what releases oxytocin may feel counter-intuitive, but perhaps by being conscious of our tendency to shut down, we can rather take the reigns and do something that will benefit us far more in the long run. While solitude can be a balm, what may quell our fears far more effectively is non-verbal connection. Exchanging a simple massage with our partner, or cuddling together in front of a fire. This is one of the benefits a loving relationship confers – huge helpings of healing oxytocin.

But it does not make a difference only after being stressed; it also pre-emptively reduces the fear response in the amygdala. By activating the social engagement system of the pre-frontal cortex – the seat of self-awareness and the same part of the brain that gets strengthened through meditation – oxytocin becomes the neurochemical foundation of resilience.

When someone is *primed* to feel safe, loved and connected before they experience a stressor, their brains are remarkably less reactive to stress. A strong and healthy pre-frontal cortex does this pre-empting by growing neuronal fibres down to the amygdala to carry GABA (gamma amino butyric acid), which quells the fear response. While the rest of the neocortex lacks effective access to the limbic (emotional) brain, the bottom of the pre-frontal cortex is only a few cell layers away from the amygdala.

When we generally have a sense of safety, trust, belonging and connection, we become resilient. But when we are in constant conflict, or stuck in a loveless relationship, the odds are stacked against us, and it may be time to make a drastic change. Harsh or critical parenting, or a lack of love in general, is a recipe for raising children ill-equipped to handle life's stressful challenges.

Fortunately, any act of kindness, or even kind thoughts, will raise the neurochemical oxytocin profile. In this way, caring for others is the best self-care there is, and feeling compassion for the suffering and distress of others, helps us heal. Research on compassion only started in the early years of the 21st century, but already a large body of evidence correlates those with higher levels of compassion with having a multitude of benefits over those who do not. Our capacity for self-compassion has also been shown to buffer anxiety and increase psychological wellbeing, while decreasing neurosis.[22] Neuroscientists are finding that even thinking about, imagining or remembering being loved or feeling compassionate connection releases oxytocin. It is no surprise

---

[22] Neff, Kirkpatrick, & Rude. *Journal of Research in Personality*, 2007

that traditional Buddhist compassion practices like tonglen and loving-kindness (*metta*) meditation are becoming accepted forms of therapy.

Angel of Love

Acceptance is the crux of compassion. Without an attitude of acceptance, we find ourselves stuck in judgmental narcissism. The suffering of others becomes their own fault, and we wash our hands of it. The faults of others loom large as we blind ourselves to our own.

What is harder to wash our hands of, is our grudges. We easily remember manoeuvres against us, and carry our resentments as a righteous duty. And so the Sentinel keeps itself employed – if you are hostile towards someone or something in your mind, you can reasonably anticipate a hostile reaction, a reprisal. Whether our enemies are real or, say, phantoms created by the media, the anticipation of attack keeps a mental kernel of fear firmly in place.

By carrying this kernel of fear we harm only ourselves, not our perceived enemies. To finally face and pacify our fears we must also learn to forgive. The process of forgiveness may not be easy, but resentment and hostility are the last vestiges of the fearful mind. Forgiving those who have (or who we perceive to have) wronged us, is one of the most challenging tests in "letting go of oneself."

It is a pre-requisite for bringing the Sentinel's festival of fear to an end. Of course the Sentinel will rationalize, and say it serves a purpose. It keeps us on red alert, ready to defend or attack. Because that is much easier than the alternative – to forgive and to love. The Sentinel prefers to lament all shortcomings. Lament first. Love later.

Such an orientation is sadly contagious. It is even conveyed chemically – when we are stressed we give off alarm pheromones that can subconsciously trigger the fear centres in the brains of others.[23] These are fearful times, with much to make us run for cover and batten down the hatches. Why put others at ease, when we can put them on edge? People are disappointing, and the end is surely nigh.

With such views, whether accurate or in error, we can spread fear in the world. Or we can drop the whole show and learn to love, despite it all. Because when you boil it right down, fear, stress, anxiety and even anger – all apparently negative emotions – arise because we *care*. The stronger the emotion, the more we care. And caring is the

---

[23] Mujica-Parodi. *PLOS ONE*, 2009

essence of compassion.

The German word for compassion is *Mitleid*, which translates as "suffering" (*leid*) "with" (*mit*). It means being willing to feel the suffering of others, and being in touch with our own emotional vulnerability and distress. And so this is where the journey brings us – where the Angel of Fear forces us to arrive. To see – to feel – that under all the stress and fear and anxiety, resides compassion. Right at the core of the human condition.

The Buddhist equivalent of the angel is the bodhisattva, and of all the bodhisattvas, Avalokiteshvara is the most celebrated. With Masculine and Feminine in perfect balance, the androgynous Avalokiteshvara with his/her two extra arms like angels' wings is the symbol of absolute, enlightened compassion. In China this Lord of Love came to be portrayed as a woman, the goddess Kuan-Yin, who cradles the symbol of the soul in her arms.

In Tibetan tantric practice, the visualization of Avalokiteshvara serves as a support for the mind's attention in meditation. The bodhisattva's rainbow body, like a reflection in water, represents the empty, open aspect of the awakened mind. The bodily transparency transcends the solidification of concepts – including the idea that the angel is "out there," separate from us.

"When angels visit us," says the poet Mary Baker Eddy, "we do not hear the rustle of wings, nor feel the feathery touch of the breast of a dove; but we know their presence by the love they create in our hearts."

LET'S DO IT ♦ Metta Meditation

Negative thoughts and emotions often result from an excessive preoccupation with ourselves, and traditional Buddhist loving-kindness meditation has been shown in research studies to be an effective antidote to depression and anxiety. Compassion is a trait that can be developed. Known as *metta* meditation, it develops the capacity for compassion, and can be practised by anyone, regardless of religious affiliation. Essentially it cultivates love.

This meditation can be done anywhere as long as you are not distracted by the sounds or activities around you, and can take anywhere from 5 minutes, to a full 45 minutes. It will be most effective as a regular practice, perhaps upon waking and before going to sleep. Regular practice has a cumulative effect and increases the benefits. It can also be done any time you feel it would help you, even at your desk at work.

Remember, it is not about getting rid of any other emotions, but simply becoming more spacious within, to allow all emotions to be as they are – to stop fighting our own minds.

My free *Still Life* album, available at *albertbuhr.com*, includes a guided *metta* meditation, but the basic formula is as follows:

1. Begin with yourself. Calm the mind and heart by taking a few deep breaths. Recall the words of Plato: "Be kind, for everyone you meet is fighting a hard battle." Let that consideration of kindness start with yourself. Generate warm, gentle, loving feelings for yourself. Say: May I be safe from harm. May I be happy just as I am. May I be peaceful with whatever is happening. May I care for myself, and feel joy.

2. Then, from yourself, mentally move out spaciously into your immediate surroundings. Include every living being within the circle of your kind-hearted love, and say: May all beings who are near me feel safe, content, at peace and free from suffering.

3. As you feel your immediate surroundings fill with the power of your capacity for kindness and love, move on, expanding slowly from one stage to the next: to the whole neighbourhood, the province, the country, the continent, until you envelop the entire planet. Visualize all creatures, from the high mountains down into the deep sea, and send them these vibrations of loving kindness – the genuine, heartfelt wish that all beings experience deep wellbeing and total freedom from stress.

4. Finally, visualize Earth, spinning within the vast, mysterious universe, and end by expanding the sense of your loving kindness to fill the entire cosmos. Say: May all living beings everywhere be fulfilled and experience profound wellbeing.

LET'S DO IT ♦ Compassionate Communication

When conflict rears its ugly head, it is primetime for mindfulness and compassion! It is all very well to feel kindly disposed toward people in general, but when we stumble into rocky terrain (or find ourselves thrust there quite innocently), it will save us a world of distress if we can apply a few communication strategies. For ease of recollection in the heat of the moment, I recommend you step out of habitual egocentric responses, and SHIFT the conversation onto a different track:

S – Say nothing! This first step is a skill that can take years to master. When you suddenly find yourself in a confrontation, *do not* immediately grab the ball and run with it. Instead, take a moment, and *do and say nothing*. Allow the awkward silence, and feel the sting without immediately trying to defend against the feeling. The impulse to defend usually causes lashing out unskilfully, which threatens your integrity. Take a few breaths, and remind yourself of the next step in SHIFT.

H – "How are you feeling?" In confrontation, our first impulse tends to be an egocentric contraction: "How very dare you!" Above all, we want to be *right*, and therefore we *must* demonstrate, for all the world to see, that the other person is *wrong*. And we must do this immediately. We are quickly defensive and acutely focused on ourselves.

Instead, try to connect with what the other person is feeling. Reflect back: "You seem hurt." Or: "You seem angry." Try to uncover as much as you can about how they feel, and don't be afraid to ask: "How are you feeling (about that)?"

Try not to content yourself with an analysis. For example: "I feel like you never take me seriously..." That is an analysis. "I feel betrayed." That is also an analysis. Try instead to boil it down to the very basic feeling in the body: sad, afraid, hurt, furious. Allow them to feel that, and acknowledge that you recognize how they feel. Try to feel that emotion if you can, even if just for a moment. It will completely shift the energy between you, because the other person will feel fully acknowledged.

I – "I can tell you really care about..." This is a powerful step. You may have received some nasty negativity. But by focussing on what is underneath the other person's annoyance or distress, by discerning what it is they *really care* about, you create a powerful reminder of the other person's basic, inherent goodness. They will feel understood.

F – Find the need. If the previous steps haven't already naturally led to a resolution, try to discover what need underlies the person's complaint. What is it they want from you? Consideration? Respect? Leaving the toilet seat down? Seeing the person's need usually brings clarity and shows the way forward, and how to resolve feelings that have been stirred up. Of course you're not obliged to meet their needs, but perhaps there is a compromise. Now that expectations are out in the open, you can negotiate.

T – Troubleshoot. If none of the steps above have helped, it is possible that you are dealing with someone who is passive-aggressive. They will appear to have no feelings, and when asked, they will deny feeling anything and remain steadfastly in analysis. In such cases, it may be helpful to shift your focus from *content* to *process*. Instead of getting entangled in *what* they said (content), find your curiosity for *why* and *how* they have said it (process). You could simply ask: "Why do you say (it like) that?" This step demonstrates deep mindfulness – instead of reacting to the content, you are stepping back and trying to see the hidden agenda. The content (*what* they say) is naturally magnetic – even a moment of not getting pulled in is a great step in the right direction. Shifting focus from content to process also shifts the focus back to them. Stick to curiosity and questions, rather than statements.

LET'S DO IT ♦ On-the-Spot Tonglen

Tonglen is a powerful meditational antidote to egocentricity. Taught in India and taken to Tibet a thousand years ago, the Dalai Lama, who is said to practise tonglen every day, has said of the technique: "Whether this meditation really helps others or not, it gives me peace of mind. Then I can be more effective, and the benefit is immense."

I have found it one of the most effective mind-training techniques.

Initially you may feel some resistance to the practice, because it dramatically turns the Sentinel's orientation around 180 degrees. It takes only a few seconds, but truly broadens perspective. Here is how:

Anytime you see someone suffering, think, "Just like me, they want to be happy." Then inhale their suffering in the imagined form of black smoke, and exhale white light to them, picturing that you are sending everything that will ease their suffering. You can do this from one breath, to one hundred, and no one needs to know – stealth visualization!

You can also use on-the-spot tonglen on strong feelings that arise, like frustration or fear. Take a moment to feel the emotion, then say, "So this is what so many other people in the world feel." Then inhale that feeling on behalf of others, and exhale the relief you would wish to feel in the imagined form of white, healing light.

11

ANGELS AND DEMONS

Nobody seemed to mind the cow chewing cud in the middle of a four-lane highway in the onslaught of rush hour. On my way to the New Delhi train station, I finally got to see, quite literally, what it means to be as calm as a Hindu cow.

The next morning I arrived at Mcleod Ganj, a tranquil village in the Himalayan foothills, and the seat of the Tibetan government in exile. A diverse group of people – lay Westerners, monastics and yogis – were gathering in the Kangra valley of northern India for a rare event. For three days His Holiness the 17th Karmapa would give transmissions on the powerful meditation practice of *chöd*.

Originally propagated in Tibet during the 11th century by the yogini Machig Labdrön, it combines tantric visualization with melodious chanting to the beat of *damaru* drums. Realization in *chöd* is said to result in complete freedom from fear. *Chöd* literally means "cutting through," and involves the imagined cutting up of one's own body as an offering to demons.

This may sound shocking to western ears. Thanks to our Abrahamic inheritance, and with the inhuman horrors of the Puritan witch hunts in England and Salem, the West has had an inflexible attitude toward the idea of demons. But the word *demon* actually originates with the ancient notion of the *daemon* – an unseen personal guide or helpmeet on the path to our deeper destiny, our sense of purpose in life. A guardian spirit. Angels and daemons, then, are not so different. But the Church sought to literally demonize pagan ideas, and by Victorian times, a newfound interest in neopaganism and the god Pan saw the Church cast their demons in the mould of a horned, goat-like image.

In Tibetan traditions, demons are not deemed evil, but are simply disruptive forces, troubled and mischievous. In *chöd*, the "demons" represent our fears, addictions and other hindrances. In a deeper sense, *chöd* means cutting through our egocentric fixations and adopting an attitude of radical, unconditional acceptance.[24] It capitalizes on the paradox that, by honouring and surrendering to our symptoms and so-called "pathologies," through mentally personifying them in the form of demons and giving them the full attention for which they clamour, we effect transformation and liberation.

The poet Rilke wrote, "Perhaps everything terrible in us is, in its deepest being, something helpless needing our help." The monstrous fear I endured, with its abysmal bouts of depression, was indeed terrible. But I had to learn that nothing is ever so clear cut. Beauty and terror, hope and fear, angels and demons, are not polar opposites, but matters of perspective.

In the West, hope is held in high esteem, deemed almost angelic. In Tibet, on the other hand, the words for hope and fear are commonly combined into one word. Hope and fear are seen to be cut from the same cloth. Both feed on the future.

My struggle through the dark night involved both hope and self-judgment. Eventually I lost the battle and, like Jacob, had to surrender, which brought a new dawn. I learnt about the power of acceptance, and was thankfully forced to return to meditation training. That dawn heralded an increase in consciousness, and a greater capacity for love. I believe I have become more self-accepting, and thereby more honest with others. It changed my life for the better in so many ways – seldom how I had thought it should look. I learnt how to steer by letting go of the controls. The Angel of Fear led me to acceptance, and taught me not to reduce my panic and anxiety to mere demons. I found freedom in the shift from "my will" to "Thy will," and opened myself to the angel's message – life is not meant to serve me; it is the other way around.

Feeding Demons

How easily we mistake the Angel of Fear for a demon. Tennessee Williams said, "If I got rid of my demons, I'd lose my angels." In learning to accept our demons, we may find angels in disguise.

---

[24] For more on this esoteric practice, see *Feeding Your Demons* by Lama Tsultrim Allione. 2008

There is even a biological correlation here. When I suffered with anxiety, I wished there were a way to get rid of my amygdala; brain surgery seemed a bright idea. But the latest neuroscience is beginning to show that the amygdala doesn't just register varieties of fear – it also reacts to good news. In fact, by learning to promote love, truth and beauty, in ourselves and in the world, we can nurture what has been called "a joyful amygdala." What's more, scientists now suspect that the amygdala may be at the heart of compassion.

The message of this book boils down to two words – acceptance and compassion. They are two sides of the same coin, and the rest is simply exhibits A through Z. Acceptance requires understanding, and some assurances. I tried to show that some reputable traditions, and some very serious people, are in accord on the subject.

The particulars of the journey are up to you. I have simply pointed out some signposts and given a general orientation.

In the study of stress under extreme conditions, three factors were shown to be vital for those who survived the Nazi concentration camps during WWII. The first is *comprehensibility* – making sense of one's experience. The second is *manageability* – having the resources to meet and manage the demands on your system. The third is *meaningfulness* – the sense that these demands are challenges in which you can find meaning. My aim, and my sincere hope, is that this book has given you at least a taste of all three factors.

Comprehensibility comes from the right knowledge and understanding of stress and anxiety, and fear in general. We have looked at the physiology of stress in the brain and body, and unpacked the underlying fictions that feed our fears and create our stress-producing habits. In this regard, knowledge really is power.

Manageability comes through practise of the exercises, as well as getting adequate sleep, water, physical exercise and nutrition. If you would like more help, I recommend my *Still Life* album of guided meditations to induce the relaxation response, freely available at *albertbuhr.com*. When practised repeatedly, all these have a cumulative effect to help heal your nervous system and build your resilience.

I have suggested some pathways to a sense of meaningfulness by considering that stress or anxiety is a call to transformation. Viewing ourselves through the prism of the medical paradigm has proven unhelpful for many people, and the reductionist ideology often underlying the conventional medical view precludes deeper meanings. Re-imagining our apparent maladies in the light of a larger paradigm allows us to regain a sense of soulfulness.

It also helps heal our split from nature. Whether through astronomy or entomology, hiking or nutrition, any reconnection to mother nature is a step in the right direction, and breaks the entrancement with the economic machine. It is no accident that Eden – that psychological paradise of union and harmony, a symbol for enlightenment – is a garden. Or that nirvana is called True Nature. Or that the Buddhist angel that specializes in the quelling of fear is depicted as green.

Acceptance is a prerequisite for opening the mind to vaster views, and the eyes to the wonder in the ordinary things we take for granted. Acceptance is a powerful life practice, a paradox that only *seems* passive but is so much more. It is a way back and through, a letting go and a finding.

It brings peace, and in the end, you might just find, it gives birth – to a faith in angels.

God Speaks by Rainer Maria Rilke

God speaks to each of us as he makes us,
then walks with us silently out of the night.

These are the words we dimly hear:

You, sent out beyond your recall,
go to the limits of your longing.
Embody me.

Flare up like flame
and make big shadows I can move in.

Let everything happen to you: beauty and terror.
Just keep going. No feeling is final.
Don't let yourself lose me.

Nearby is the country they call life.
You will know it by its seriousness.

Give me your hand.

Appendix A

"I'M GOING SLIGHTLY MAD" *BY ROB NAIRN*

Going mad – a scary phrase. A surprising number of meditation practitioners fear, at some point in their practice, that they are going mad. "Losing their marbles." I'm always mildly intrigued by this term because I have heard it so often that my mind now spontaneously presents an image of some secret repository where all those lost marbles have ended up.

But when it is happening to you it is not so funny, so let's see if we can get a workable perspective on the subject.

IF YOU THINK YOU ARE, YOU'RE NOT

My first and most important observation is that those people who think they are going mad are almost always, by that very fact, demonstrating sanity. I say this because most forms of so-called insanity that I have encountered involve loss of touch with external reality and a withdrawal into some form of delusional condition. This latter can also be caused by an overwhelming upsurge of unconscious material that swamps the conscious, functioning mind and impairs its capacity to relate accurately and rationally with the outside world. The result of this is usually loss of perspective, but most importantly, the subjects typically do not realise it is happening. They don't think they are "going mad." They would believe in the reality of their delusional world, see and hear things, and project their unconscious contents onto the outside world with an inflexible conviction that the problem is out there. Which is why you cannot reason with them.

So to be blunt, "mad" people usually don't think they are mad, whereas people who think they are going mad are clearly not, because they still have enough objective awareness of themselves and the outside world to prove sanity.

But this does not mean that we are always perfectly balanced. Sometimes in meditation practice, intense and powerful shifts within our energy systems can happen and these can produce disturbing effects because they push us beyond our normal boundaries of experience – into areas of ourselves that are new, strange, unfamiliar.

This can be scary.

Thus far, I have talked only in generalities in an attempt to sketch the overall perspective. I have also not tried to define mad, and am not sure that I will, because perhaps if I do, it will lead to the conclusion that we are all already mad.

Not Psychology

Psychologists have extensive lists of criteria that they use as diagnostic guides. These help them classify people who present emotional or mental disturbances. On this basis they are able to prescribe treatment. I wish to make it clear that I am not going there. What I offer here is rather a series of observations and conclusions based on my experience over the years with thousands of people engaged in intensive meditation practice over extended periods of time – in retreat. It is common under these conditions for people to start "cooking." One of my main jobs has been to help them understand, accept and grow through the "cooking" process, which is usually important, creative and valuable.

So I am not claiming to align anything I say here to clinical perspectives.

The Scenario

Here's how I see it.

We humans have limitless potential, which is present constantly – at every moment, right now, right here. We fail to realize or experience this because we are locked into a limited and rigid view of ourselves. This view has become our reality and blocks out any greater possibility. It has created a matrix into which our energy has become magnetized and frozen. As this happens, the configuration, which is unique to each one of us, becomes familiar, comfortable – even if often painful – and safe: the safety of the known. It is so rigid, inflexible and constant that it becomes what we call reality – this is my reality; this is what I am; this is me. But it's not real.

Have you ever heard a sound in the dark of night and concluded that someone was there? Maybe you lay rigid with fear, waiting for something to happen. At last you found the courage to move and turn the light on… and there was a piece of paper moving in a breeze. Most of us can think of similar instances.

Now, can you put yourself back into that space where you lay in fear? Can you recapture that conviction of absolute reality that gripped your mind? Can you recall how unquestioningly you lay there in the dark with your heart pounding?

And then – can you contrast the relief and sense of freedom when you discovered it was not true, not real?

This is an echo of our human condition. We are lying in the dark trapped in terrified torpor by the belief that this condition is reality. And that belief is powerful enough to hold us like a vice. No amount of reasoning, learning, theorizing or intellectualizing will free us from it. Somehow we have to switch the light on. That can only be done experientially.

This is why we engage in mind-training. When we do this through something like mindfulness practice, we unwittingly activate changes in the deeper layers of our energy systems. This process of change is not consciously, intentionally initiated or directed. It is an unknown and unexpected consequence of our training efforts.

These deeper energies are more powerful than the surface layers where we dwell; they move like subterranean magma, forcing themselves to the surface, finding geological fault lines and moving up them. This analogy works well because we know that subterranean activity can be felt at the surface in the form of earth tremors, quakes and other movements. Finally, there might be a volcano – dramatic and terrifying – red hot lava spewing out and exploding into the heights.

In our practice, the deep energies are demanding that we begin the process of facing the reality of what is really here and letting go of our rigid, limited belief in something less.

Experientially this can manifest in a variety of ways. The most common is for our repression systems to come under pressure. This often leads to an intensified awareness of negative, conflicting and painful emotions that we have spent our lives denying and trying not to feel. Our inner defences weaken and crumble, and strong repressed states can begin to surface. When this happens it is common for people to feel that unusually strong and terrible feelings are assailing them from outside. The surface mind will typically view this as disastrous because it is a manifestation of exactly what we have unconsciously defined as bad and wrong and tried to turn away from.

This is the point where many people decide they are going mad (or being assailed by demons) because there is usually a sense of losing control and being swamped by terrible feelings that should not be there, and seem to have come from some independent, external source. Then typically, what is a healthy growing process can be met with terror and a frantic effort to re-repress.

This is stating the situation at its most extreme and dramatic. Few people seem to have such powerful manifestations, but many have milder versions that more or less follow this pattern. In the beginning of our training these "movements of energy" can be alarming for several reasons.

Firstly, they are involuntary and outside our control. This in itself can be alarming because it constitutes an inner manifestation of something beyond the familiar, and is thus viewed as dangerous.

Secondly, they often contradict our rigid view of how we are or should be. Most of us have unrealistic self-images strongly influenced by the belief that we are only safe, acceptable and OK if we manifest sanitized personalities free from negative traits. These "movements" therefore unsettle us at a deep level and seem to demolish our carefully constructed – but ramshackle – reality.

Also, most of us know very little about ourselves and usually exist in a state of denial about our negative and painful states, and ignorance about the activities of the unconscious and subliminal layers of our minds. As a result, we often feel as though we are living with a stranger – one who seems to be more powerful than "we" are, and frighteningly unpredictable. This can leave us with a sense of apprehension, waiting for something to go wrong. When unpredictable changes happen, the mind could therefore jump to the conclusion that *this is it! Now the catastrophe is finally upon me.* This can set off an escalation of fear and feelings of "losing it."

This doesn't exhaust the range of possibilities, and many people would present their own unique configurations. But if we understand in principle what can and often does happen, then when our own unique experience arises, we can go through it without feeling that something has gone wrong.

The Principle

It seems that spiritual and psychological growth involves inner change – to state the obvious. But what does this mean? Essentially, having to face and compassionately accept ourselves as we are. This may sound surprising. You may ask – how is that a change? It's a change from how most people are – non-self-aware, in denial about unwanted states, and largely non-self-accepting.

This facing and compassionately accepting usually begins as an idea, but when we do a lot of practice we begin to discover that our inner environment is under the constant scrutiny of our preference systems. This causes us, without realizing it, to divide our thoughts and feelings into categories of good and bad. Good is to be approved and encouraged. Bad is to be denied and got rid of. Since we cannot get rid of parts of ourselves, we repress. Repression is supported by denial, so the official story becomes that the feelings in question do not exist. There is a pushing down and bottling up involved.

This strategy (which is unconscious) can produce a semblance of harmony and balance in the personality as long as there is sufficient energy available to maintain the blocks, and provided the volume of repressed material is not too great and dynamic.

But repressed material never goes away by itself. It remains locked into the deeper layers of consciousness. Although we may be in denial about it, we will nevertheless constantly feel it in the form of a generalized sense of unease or anxiety – like we might get if we walked into a room and realized that someone was hiding there. The person cannot be seen but we sense the presence and know that they are dangerous. This feeling of being in danger will be generalized – nearly always there but we cannot actually put our finger on it and say, "Oh, this is the problem."

So we are never able to deal with it, and generally project it onto others. This makes us troublesome to be around and will gradually lead to isolation from others.

Under intensive training, the barriers of denial and repression could, as mentioned earlier, begin to collapse. This can cause feelings of alarm and threat. It can seem that outside forces are gathering and bursting upon us. We may single out individuals upon whom we project blame, trying to make them responsible for all our problems. This is very common in group situations.

When this happens the mark of a true practitioner is that he or she remains stable – i.e. not reacting – long enough to realize that the problem is coming from their own mind and not from someone else. The person then takes responsibility for the projections and compassionately learns to accept themselves as they are with all the flaws and weaknesses.

This is significant, sane and mature behaviour under conditions where most people might go off the rails a bit. It is difficult to do because most of us have strong unseen patterns of dumping our unresolved states on others, and blaming and attacking them. This example illustrates how we can drift towards potential madness, but how we can check ourselves and use the experience instead to produce a positive outcome – that of compassionately accepting, allowing the feeling to surface fully and be integrated. This is what produces growth.

The mad response is to clamp the lid down more fiercely and resort to increasingly dramatic projections, all the while insisting that there is nothing wrong with "me," because it is all out there; others are wrong and are trying to do bad things to me.

At the end of the day, it seems to me that most of us are constantly moving back and forth along an invisible spectrum between so-called sanity and madness.

Is it an old Yorkshire comment by a husband to his wife? "It seems to me that everyone in the world is mad except thy and I, and even thy be mad sometimes."

Appendix B

ORIENTATION FOR SEVERE ANXIETY

Anxiety can do you no harm. The heart palpitations are not dangerous. The sense of unreality (or depersonalization) is normal. Even while it feels like you are about to be annihilated, it is all smoke and mirrors. Symptoms can be numerous and strange, but they all have perfectly rational explanations. Learn not to be too impressed by symptoms, whatever they might be.

You are perfectly safe.

That said, get a basic medical check-up anyway, because this is the best way to dispel all those doubts. (If you have anxiety, you may easily be a bit of a hypochondriac!) Doctors are trained to detect physical conditions that may cause your anxiety, and these are invariably benign and easily treated. If they give you the all-clear and tell you that you are suffering from anxiety, believe them.

Trying to get rid of anxiety keeps it alive, adding stress to stress. Learning to accept, removes this additional load of stress and thereby allows your nervous system to heal naturally. Unless we are unwittingly doing something to prevent it, the body will always move towards balance.

As long as you can get out of the way of its healing, through acceptance and by following some of the simple recommendations in this book, your nervous system will naturally heal. You have kept it out of balance without realizing it. Learning acceptance will fix all that.

This healing and rebalancing of the nervous system is a slow process, and will teach you patience. When you break a leg, you get a cast and crutches, and you do not use that leg for six weeks. But we cannot put our nervous systems in gypsum and press pause on their use – we need to use it every day, and so it may take longer to heal. This healing is so slow that you will often think it is not happening.

It is happening.

There are practical and physical things you can do to speed up the process. In some cases, considerably. But they work cumulatively, over a period of weeks, or even months – not on the spot. There are no quick-fix magic bullets. None that work in the long run, anyway. The quicker the fix, the sooner the setback.

During the months of recovery, you will experience what are called setbacks many, many times. This is absolutely par for the course. During a setback, you will usually feel you have lost any gains you have made. You haven't – drowning in deep ocean or drowning in shallow water still feels like drowning. Just because you cannot see the shore does not mean it isn't getting closer.

Setbacks seem like obstacles, but they are opportunities for learning patience and practising acceptance. Welcome them. They are in fact "healing crises" or "healing reactions." They are necessary and will deepen your mind training.

Try not to give your fears so much credit. What seems real and serious is rarely more than the mind playing tricks. Remember, the Sentinel – that part of the mind always on the lookout for potential threats – has everything to gain from making you believe you are in mortal danger. It operates on the motto: better safe than sorry. That rustle in the grass? The Sentinel has nothing to lose from having you believe it is a tiger, and not the wind. Your task is not to trust it. Almost all your fearful thoughts are just that – thoughts. Don't let your thoughts or your physical symptoms impress you.

Stress is mostly created in the mind. That is why many of the exercises in this book are mental. Do them! Refer to them again and again. They *will* help you. And keep practising your chosen relaxation techniques, as provided on my *Still Life* album that functions as a companion to this book, freely available at *albertbuhr.com*.

Although you may often think that you're going it alone, millions of people have experienced what you are experiencing. I have helped people who could hardly smile, and whose anxiety was so severe during the workshops that they literally had to hold onto their seats. They believed that they would never heal. And I have seen these same people make full recoveries. Remember, you are not alone!

"Be patient and tough," says Ovid in the *Metamorphoses*. "One day this pain will be useful to you." Take heart. All really will be well.

Appendix C

RECOMMENDED READING

Beyond Fear by **Dorothy Rowe** – this is the bible for an alternative, critical look at the over-medicalization of "psychopathology," whether it be depression, anxiety or psychosis. Immensely insightful and informative.

Care of the Soul and *The Soul's Religion* by **Thomas Moore** – classics in the tradition of depth psychology.

Diamond Mind by **Rob Nairn** – for authentic, in-depth and down-to-earth meditation instruction without the Buddhist baggage. Rob is the angel of acceptance.

Full Catastrophe Living by **Jon Kabat-Zinn** – a pioneer in the field of mindfulness and stress-reduction for people living with anxiety, depression and pain.

Healing Without Freud or Prozac by **David Servan-Schreiber** – a renowned psychiatrist prefers some natural methods for healing anxiety and depression, like "heart coherence," acupuncture and omega-3s.

How to Live Dangerously by **Warwick Cairns** – a light-hearted look at our culture of fear and obsessive risk-avoidance.

Ironic Effects of Trying to Relax under Stress by **Daniel M. Wegner, Alexis Broome and Stephen J. Blumber** – an interesting research paper on "paradoxical anxiety" from the Department of Psychology at the University of Virginia, which concludes that full acceptance is key.

***Psychology of the Future* by Stanislav Grof** – one of the founders of transpersonal psychology places the idea of "madness" in a whole new light, arguing that even psychosis is often an (admittedly disturbing) "healing reaction."

***Swamplands of the Soul* by James Hollis** – an insightful and reassuring guide through our emotional difficulties from a renowned Jungian analyst. All his books are treasures.

***The Compassionate Mind* by Paul Gilbert** – a brilliant, authoritative book from a famous neuroscientist and clinical psychologist who looks at the science of healing the mind through compassion, and offers many practical exercises.

***The Happiness Trap* by Russ Harris** – an easy yet thorough introduction to the principles and practices of the highly effective Acceptance and Commitment Therapy.

***The Joy of Living* by Mingyur Rinpoche** – a prodigal meditation master in the Kagyu tradition talks candidly about his struggles with anxiety and panic that lasted many years, and how he overcame these through acceptance and meditation practice in remarkably short time. A good introduction to practical Buddhism and meditation.

***The Magnesium Miracle* by Carolyn Dean** – an MD and naturopath celebrates the healing power of this amazing mineral.

***The Power of Now* by Eckhart Tolle** – a teacher with the gift of clarity and simplicity, Tolle also once suffered from really severe anxiety until his remarkable breakthrough.

***The Soul's Code* by James Hillman** – an unusually accessible classic from the great father of archetypal psychology, on finding value and purpose in life.

When Love Meets Fear **by David Richo** – a therapist's insightful, warm-hearted meditation on the effect that love and compassion have on fear.

When Things Fall Apart **and** ***The Places that Scare You*** **by Pema Chödron** – a fresh and radical approach that really makes a difference. Her chapter *Fearlessness and Death* (in *When Things Fall Apart*) is completely unlike most self-help stuff you come across, and is paradoxically effective.

ACKNOWLEDGMENTS

This book would not have been possible without the kindness and generosity of friends, family and strangers.

Firstly, I am deeply indebted to the many authors I have never met, but who helped me out of a dark hole thanks to their written works and websites, and their dedication to helping others find acceptance – those not included in the Recommended Reading appendix but worth special mention are Paul David of anxietynomore.co.uk, and the late Dr Claire Weekes.

I thank Rob Nairn for his invaluable contribution to this book, and his encouragement to develop my first workshop. He was instrumental in giving me the confidence needed to further my ambitions to help others who suffer.

Gratitude to Mignon Corder and the management of the Cape Town Samye Dzong for the platform to present my courses for many years. Thanks to Charlotte Harmse for assistance in organizing upcoming events and preparing the shrine room so many times. Thanks also to psychologist Lilly Teggin for overseeing my very first course.

I am grateful to lucid dreaming teacher Charley Morley for being the first to suggest taking on the challenge, and for his friendship. Also to Walton Pantland for being a trusted, longstanding friend who read and supplied notes on the first draft.

A deep bow of gratitude to Erika van Greunen for her great kindness in helping me gain sponsorship to receive teachings from His Holiness the Karmapa and HH the Dalai Lama in India. I doff the proverbial hat also to the generosity of the actual sponsors, both known and anonymous.

Finally, I am grateful daily to Dr J.H. Buhr for keeping me afloat and free of danger, and for Lorraine Buhr's tireless guidance and always helping without hesitation. An especial thanks for her thorough and skilful editing of this book.

A warm embrace to my partner Zo for her faith and calm, her perceptiveness and encouragement, her patience and love.

ABOUT THE AUTHOR

Since recovering naturally from a prolonged period of debilitating anxiety, Albert Buhr has travelled the world to learn the best methods for subduing the stress response, from neuroscience seminars at Oxford to holotropic breathwork on the beaches of Mexico; from meditation in the monasteries of Meteora, to learning the esoteric practice of *chöd* in the foothills of the Himalayas.

Endorsed by Dr Mark Williams (originator of Mindfulness-Based Cognitive Therapy), as well as author Rob Nairn, he has facilitated at a diverse range of companies, from banks to Bostik. As a member of Harvard's Langer Mindfulness Institute he has taken his workshops as far afield as the Caribbean, has been an editor for the University of Aberdeen's Mindfulness Association, as well as the daily mindfulness coach for Oprah's online platform in South Africa.

A former novice monk, Albert is passionate about promoting practical and contemplative methods to balance the nervous system and help others find their natural capacity for inner calm.

AUDIO DOWNLOAD

Visit the author's website to download his *Still Life* album of guided restorative practices. It offers a few of the world's most powerful healing practices to balance the nervous system and build the body's natural capacity for calm. Practised regularly, they have a cumulative effect over time to increase your resilience and end your stress and anxiety. Tracks can be downloaded individually or all together, or simply streamed. This is completely FREE.

albertbuhr.com

www.ingramcontent.com/pod-product-compliance
Lightning Source LLC
Chambersburg PA
CBHW051806040426
42446CB00007B/544